A History of the Allen and Wilson Families

Howard W. Allen

DEDICATION

In Memory of my Grandfather
Robert Wilson

CONTENTS

ACKNOWLEDGMENTS

I am especially indebted to my wife Lorie Jenner Allen who has been especially encouraging and supportive as I have undertaken this genealogical project. She has also been invaluable because of her exceptional skills with software, computers and the intricacies of publication, not to mention the fact that she's also an insightful critic to whom I have learned to pay attention. Thanks as well to my son Mark Wilson Allen who read this manuscript and revealed some genuine and ongoing interest in family history, especially as it is revealed in DNA analysis. He has provided many insightful suggestions and criticisms.

And, thanks to my Grandfather, Robert Wilson, whose drawing of his early home became the cover of this book and whose Memoir encouraged my interest in family history.

CHAPTER 1

INTRODUCTION

Over the years since I retired, I have worked on and off with the popular genealogy company Ancestry.com to create a family genealogical history. I quickly determined that this was a very complicated and almost impossible project. In three generations there are 14 ancestors and in four generations there are 30, and I know very little about most of them except what I have in the family genealogical tree in Ancestry.com. I do have more information about the descendants of Josiah Allen and Winifred Ingram and of Lewis Wilson and Martha Ann Crunk. As a result, I will provide genealogical tables and other information for as many of the North American born ancestors depending on my limited knowledge, but I will focus on the Josiah Allen and Lewis Wilson families. There is little doubt that almost all of my ancestors, before arriving in North America, were of Anglo-Saxon descent. I have the results of my DNA which bear this out as follows: 42% Scotland, 42% England, 12% Ireland, 2% Wales and 1% Norway. Probably the Scotch-Irish background originates primarily in the Wilson family, and most of the others from northern England and Scotland.

I should also point out that I have done little research beyond what I can do at home on my computer and on the basis of the materials that have been passed down to me from both sides of the family. My mother, Helen Wilson Allen, was the last surviving member of both families, and somehow a lot of documents and photographs were left to her and eventually to me. I'm especially lucky to have inherited the Bible of my great-grandfather, William Bright Allen, which included in his beautiful handwriting, the exact dates of the birth of all of his children. Some obituaries were inserted into the pages of his Bible, probably by my grandmother, Laura Marsh Allen, since there was a considerable accumulation of grocery bills, postcards and other items, obviously hers, also found there.

I have also relied very heavily on the materials available in Ancestry.com. This includes information about individuals available in Ancestry from the manuscript censuses in very readable condition and from clues provided to me by Ancestry software which searches the results of the work of other researchers who have also found information about my ancestors. Through Ancestry I have also been able to access a few wills and other legal documents. Without this genealogy tool I would not have been able to accumulate information that I have without much greater time, travel and expense.

According to David Hackett Fisher in his highly regarded study of the early settlement of North America, the term Scotch-Irish is an imprecise description of the population that began to flow into the British American colonies sometime in the years around 1700 and lasted until approximately 1775. This was a movement of population from a very different part of the British Isles compared to earlier population movements. This surge originated in the northern sections of England, the southern part of Scotland near the English border, and northern, Protestant Ireland. It was an area with a long history through the Middle Ages of violence, robbery and pillage and, of course, much poverty. According to Fisher, most of the immigrants from this borderland "were farmers and farm laborers who owned no land of their own, that worked as tenants and under-tenants."[1] On the other hand, says Fischer, "they did not come from the bottom of British society." Most of this 18th century population surge traveled in family

---

[1] David Hackett Fischer, Albion's Seed. Four British Folkways in America (Oxford: Oxford University Press, 1989), 613. See also Douglas K. Meyer, Making the Heartland Quilt. A Geographical History of Settlement and Migration in Early-Nineteenth-Century Illinois (Carbondale and Edwardsville: Southern Illinois University Press, 2000), 136-168.

groups and arrived primarily in Philadelphia but also in Virginia and Charleston, South Carolina. They were not welcome in the developed sections of the British colonies. Some migrated west into the Pennsylvania frontier, as the Wilsons did, but most wandered down the unsettled mountain valleys of Appalachia into the back country of Virginia, East Tennessee, North Carolina, South Carolina, and Georgia, most of them searching for unclaimed land to farm.

CHAPTER 2

THE JOSIAH ALLEN FAMILY

The first Allen in my family line to settle in Hamilton County was Josiah Allen. His known first ancestor in North America was Gideon Allen. Gideon first appears in 1748 in the records of Johnston County, North Carolina. This information is based on the work done by Merritt E. Roberts who conducted thorough and painstaking genealogical research in Johnston County North Carolina wills, probate records and other legal documents. He published the results in 1985.[2]

Roberts found nothing about Gideon Allen before 1748, but the little I do know about early North Carolina history is that it was very sparsely settled until well after the American Revolution. Although I'm not a colonial historian, I understand that North Carolina played a limited role in the American Revolution and in the adoption of the United States Constitution of 1789. It is also the case that the upper-class plantation owners in the Tidewater region of Virginia and North and South Carolina were very contemptuous of the backwoods settlers in North Carolina in this period and later. The western counties in the Piedmont and Appalachia in North Carolina were very different from the coastal area, and there was conflict between the two sections of the state from the very earliest days of the colony. Slavery had a much more pronounced presence in the coastal region, and the western counties seemed to be regarded by the eastern counties in these early years primarily as a buffer against the Indians. There were also conflicts over ownership of land, internal improvements and in general the arrogant and authoritarian manner in which the

---

[2] Merritt E. Roberts, <u>Roberts-Allen Families and Related Families Davis, Highfill, Rogers</u> (Oliver Press Publications, 1985), 271-323.

slave–owning, coastal and more prosperous counties dominated the politics of the state. Over the decades of the 18th century a very intense resentment on the part of poor, small farmer communities in the mountainous areas of the state developed against the more prosperous, slave owning counties along the Atlantic coast.

Chances are very high that Gideon Allen arrived with little except the clothes on his back. About half of the early settlers in North America were indentured servants, convicts (the British frequently dumped prison populations into the American colonies to get rid of them until after the American Revolution when they turned to Australia), or slaves. Most of the inmates in British prisons in late the 17th and 18th centuries were incarcerated for indebtedness or very minor crimes that would not be considered crimes at all today. Primarily their problem was poverty. David Hackett Fisher believes that "remarkably few came in bondage,"[3] but he does not explain how they were able to afford passage. The Encyclopedia of American History estimates that in the Middle Colonies, particularly in the tobacco producing counties, indentured servitude of two to seven years in exchange for passage was the means of reaching America for approximately 62% to 77% of total white immigration from the end of the 17th century down to the American Revolution (1700 – 1776).[4]

The records which Merritt E. Roberts found in Johnston County indicated that Gideon Allen was probably fairly prosperous by the standards of backcountry North Carolina in the 18th century and not likely a man who had recently worked off an indentured passage. Roberts found that Gideon Allen owned more than 400 acres of land and engaged in frequent land and slave transactions. Perhaps he arrived in North Carolina with more money than most early settlers, or it is possible that he was an indentured servant who, when his indentured term expired as part of his contract, was

---

[3] Fischer, 614.

[4] Richard B. Morris and Jeffrey B. Morrie (eds.), Encyclopedia of American History (New York, 7th Edition, 1996), 750.

awarded land in the western counties. Gideon traded in land, farm stock and at least a few slaves. Roberts's findings also indicate that Gideon's sons and grandsons also traded in land, livestock and slaves.[5] He was also paid by Cumberland County to maintain a ferry for the year 1757, probably across Cape Fear River.

Gideon had a total of four sons with his wife Elizabeth: James K. Allen (1740-1787), Gideon Allen Jr. (1746-1782), Jesse Allen (1745-?), and my ancestor John Phillip Allen (1747-1796). There were at least two marriages between the Allens and the locally prominent Smith family. John Smith had established a ferry over the Neuse River which became the foundation for Smithfield, North Carolina. There were many descendants of Gideon who stayed in Johnston County and are still to be found there in 2022. There is a place a few miles southwest of Smithfield that is known as Allens Crossroads, and land deeds show that Gideon and his sons owned lands at this location south of Hannah Creek, as well as at many other locations in the county and town lots in Smithfield. There are numerous small cemeteries nearly adjacent to Allens Crossroads that hold many Allens. Gideon likely died before 1770, leaving no known will.

John Phillip Allen (1749-1797) and his wife Edith Watson (possibly born a Smith) had at least five children. He left a probated will which shows that he possessed considerable land holdings and more than a small number of slaves, with over 20 named and divided among his family. My great-great-great

---

[5] This was a pattern for small successful farmers that extended throughout the South before the end of slavery. In 1860 only approximately 33% of southerners owned any slaves and most of them owned only a few slaves and usually worked in the kitchen or fields with them. "Of the more than 8 million whites in the South in 1860 only 383,637 were slave owners. Of these, only 2,292 were large planters (holding more than 100 or more slaves)." Ibid., 746. Watson, Alan D. 1974. "The Ferry in Colonial North Carolina: A Vital Link in Transportation," The North Carolina Historical Review 51:247-260.

grandfather was William Smith Allen (1775-1832) who married Rachel Jones (1780-1829) in 1794. William lived his life in Johnston County, and was involved in numerous land transactions like his father and grandfather. They had twelve children. There is no known will for William.

Josiah Allen (1798-1855), my great grandfather and Gideon Allen's great-grandson, was born in Johnston County, North Carolina in 1798. He married Winnifred Ingram (1800-1862) in 1821. Their first child, Jincy Ann Allen, was born in 1822 and the second, William Bright Allen (my great grandfather), was born in 1824, both in Johnston County. Sometime between 1824 and 1827 Josiah and his family abandoned Johnson County and migrated West. They were accompanied by Winnifred's father, John Ingram, his wife, Catherine Sewell Ingram, and probably most members of his family. Group travel in family or church groups to the west was a very common practice. Groups provided many more hands to cope with the difficulties of travel and providing food, help in times of trouble and group morale to survive the dangers of travel in an untamed frontier where help was almost never available.

Their next child, Elizabeth Evaline Allen, was born in McNairy County, Tennessee, a county close to the Tennessee River. Although there is no way to know for sure, this probably means that they traveled overland from Johnston County to the Tennessee River and then downriver by flatboat on the Tennessee River from the very western edge of North Carolina into south-central Tennessee. Probably the most common method of transportation in the early 19th century to the American West was along the major rivers--the Mississippi, the Ohio, the Cumberland, and the Tennessee. Travel by river in those days, particularly if it included children, household goods and farm stock, was very common and far simpler by water than overland travel, even though this method of travel was also dangerous and unpredictable. David McCullough in <u>The Pioneers</u> provides a description of flatboat travel which was very common on the Ohio River in the same years:

The roof or deck of the boat is not unlike a farmyard, being covered with hay, ploughs, carts, wagons… [and] spinning wheels of the matrons were conspicuous. Even the sides of the floating- mass were loaded with the wheels of the different vehicles which themselves laid on the roof."[6]

Josiah and Winifred and John Ingram's family traveled on to Illinois, almost certainly again along the Tennessee River some time in 1829-1831. But before they traveled north, they settled temporarily in McNairy County, Tennessee. McNairy County, Tennessee is located near the Tennessee River on the Alabama border where the river turns back north after passing over the Muscle Shoals rapids. The Muscle Shoals rapids were unnavigable which would have required that they abandon their flatboat and travel overland around the rapids. It was apparently at this point that the Allen-Ingram group settled temporarily in McNairy County, Tennessee.

They probably remained in McNairy County for at least two years. Evaline was born in 1827 in McNairy County and a son, John Wright, was also born there in 1828. Their next child, Calvin Young, probably was born in Hamilton County, Illinois in 1831. A daughter, Caroline Allen, was also born in Illinois in 1832, and a son, Josephus, according to his obituary, in Macon County, Illinois in 1833. This obituary is the only document known that the Allen family was ever in Macon County, although it does appear that John Ingram's family was there.

Four years later the Allens and the Ingrams were in Hamilton County, Illinois when Penelope Allen was born in 1837. I find this part of the story the most incomprehensible. Why would the Allen and Ingram families have traveled overland from wherever they landed in Illinois across the Ohio from the

---

[6] David McCullough, The Pioneers. The Heroic Story of the Settlers Who Brought the American Ideal West (New York: Simon & Schuster, 2019), 61.

Tennessee River to central Illinois? With babies and small children? And why, then, trek back to southern Illinois in the late 1830s to settle in Hamilton County? There were roads of a sort or trails which connected the river towns to one another. In southern Illinois the most important road reached St. Louis from Shawneetown on the Ohio River and the location of one of the earliest federal land offices in Illinois.   An 1828 map of roads in Illinois indicates that while there was a rudimentary system in place at that time in the southern part of the state, there was no indication of a road to Decatur in Macon County. But despite the hazards of land travel into central Illinois, the Ingrams were in Macon County in 1830 where John Ingram was recorded as a citizen of Macon County in the 1830 Census. At that time there were six persons living in his family.   Three were males, one age 15 – 20, one age 20 – 29, and one age 50 – 59. Three were also three females in the household, one age 5 – 9, one age 10 – 14, and one age 50 – 59.[7] One of John Ingram's sons, Kinion Wright Ingram served in Company J, 5th Regiment Mounted Volunteers, Illinois Militia between 1831 and 1832 in the Blackhawk War which pretty effectively ended the Indian threat to settlement in north and central Illinois. Kinion died in Macon County in 1835 before the family moved south to Hamilton County. Roberts relates a story told to him that the Allens found Macon County too cold and were headed back to Tennessee, but decided Hamilton County would do during the trip south.

At any rate, the Ingrams and the Allens were in Hamilton County, Illinois by 1837 at the latest when Penelope was born. Josiah purchased 40 acres of land from the federal government at the General Land Office in 1838 in Shawneetown and settled in an undeveloped area a few miles west of McLeansboro. His family quickly affiliated themselves with Ten Mile Baptist Church. Josiah became very active in that church, and one record indicates that he

---

[7] I searched the 1830 Macon County Manuscript Census for Josiah Allen, but he did not appear, nor did his son William.

was the founder of the first Sunday school at Ten Mile Church.[8] Josiah and Winefred went on to have more children in Hamilton County, a total of eleven.

Josiah's oldest son, my great-grandfather, William Bright Allen (1824-1874), purchased land from the Shawneetown General Land Office several times, and lived most of his life on a small farm near Ten Mile Church in Hamilton County. He married Susan Catherine Miller (1828-1899) in 1847 in White County, Illinois. His family usually called him Bright and in one of the obituaries I have he was referred to as "Brite" Allen. He and Susan had at least 10 children, one of whom was Howard Henderson Allen (1861-1934) my grandfather.

I know very little about Susan Miller Allen. She was illiterate and signed her name with an "X" in her application for a Civil War pension after William's death. The illiteracy rate among women on the western frontier was very high. Her father, John Miller, was born in North Carolina about 1770. That's all I know about him.

The Civil War was probably the most important experience in Bright Allen's life. The war broke out in April 1861, and five months later, October 11, 1861, William Bright Allen, at the time 37 years old, enlisted in Company D, 6th Illinois cavalry at McLeansboro. His brother, James K. Allen, and cousin, Sewel Ingram, also enlisted in the same unit. Most of Company D consisted of residents of Hamilton County, including my great-grandfather Thomas Marsh. After the war, Thomas came to live on the farm next to William Bright Allen. More about him later. William and Thomas Marsh were both elected Sergeants at the time of the organization of Company D perhaps because they were

---

[8] Carol Lee Yarbrough, "The Yesterdays of Hamilton County, Illinois," carolyar.com/Illinois/Hamilton County.htm.

two of the older men in the Company.[9]

The Sixth Illinois Cavalry was organized officially at Camp Butler in November 1861 and transferred that same month to Shawneetown. Then as part of General Ulysses S. Grant's army, the Unit transferred to Paducah, Kentucky where it participated in Grant's invasion of the South along the Mississippi, Tennessee and Cumberland Rivers. Grant was not in command of the entire military operation in the West until later.

The 6th Illinois Cavalry was used primarily for scouting and chasing Confederate bands of raiders in Tennessee and Northern Mississippi. A description written by William Bright Allen in his application for a disability pension in 1869 helps describe some of the things that he experienced. He wrote that his general disability resulted

> from exposure to wet and cold weather and without tents while scouting and raiding around in West Tennessee and North Mississippi after the rebels under command of the rebel General Price and from hard service during the winter and spring of 1863.[10]

William Bright Allen was medically discharged from the hospital

---

[9] Service Record of William Bright Allen, Company D, 6th Illinois Voluntary Cavalry, Compiled Military Service Record (National Archives). Hereafter cited as CMSR and Service record of James K. Allen, Ibid.   A roster of the names of the members of Co. D, 6th Illinois Volunteer Cavalry probably at the time of organization of the unit is in Carol Lee Yarbrough, "The Yesterdays of Hamilton County, Illinois," carolyar.com/Illinois/Hamilton County.htm.

[10] Pension record of William Bright Allen, General Index to Pension Files, 1861-1934 (National Archives). A roster of the names of the members of Co. D, 6th Illinois Volunteer Cavalry probably at the time of organization of the unit is in Carol Lee Yarbrough, "The Yesterdays of Hamilton County, Illinois," carolyar.com/Illinois/Hamilton County.htm.

in LaGrange, Tennessee in 1863 and spent the rest of his life on his farm in Hamilton County. He died on December 23, 1874 and was buried in the cemetery at Ten Mile Church. His wife Susan died on July 4, 1899, and I'm sure was buried next to him in the family cemetery plot at Ten Mile Church. I obtained a Civil War monument for him and had it placed next to his parents' monument in the family cemetery plot in 2013. The plot also contains monuments to Josiah and Winifred Ingram Allen and to their son James K. Allen and his wife Eliza Jane Rice Allen. Probably others in the family are buried there as well, but there are no existing markers.

William's younger brother, James K. Allen, who at age 18 also enlisted in 1861 in Company D, served the entire war, much of it as a hospital worker and ambulance driver, which probably helped him survive the war since it would have kept him out of some direct combat. He was on duty during the famous Grierson's Raid in which Company D of the 6th Illinois Cavalry was part of a cavalry force which mounted a raid from LaGrange, Tennessee behind Confederate lines to Baton Rouge, Louisiana. This campaign was part of General Grant's overall strategy to capture Vicksburg. The plan was for Grierson's Cavalry to raid behind the lines into Western Mississippi to divert Confederate forces away from Vicksburg as Grant's Army was crossing the Mississippi River. It was the most "spectacular cavalry adventure of the war" and played a vital role in Grant's victory at Vicksburg."[11]

––––––––––––––––––––

[11] Service Record of James K. Allen, Company D, 6th Illinois Voluntary Cavalry, CMSR. James M. McPherson, <u>Battle Cry of Freedom: The Civil War Era</u> (Oxford: Oxford University Press, 1988), 628. D. Alexander Brown, <u>Grierson's Raid. A Cavalry Adventure of the Civil War</u> (Urbana: University of Illinois Press,1962). A Hollywood film, "The Horse Soldiers," starring John Wayne and William Holden, is based very loosely on Grierson's Raid but you would have little idea from the film that

William Bright's namesake nephew, William Bright Shirley, son of his older sister Jincy, enlisted in the 40th Illinois Infantry Regiment in Springfield on July 25, 1861. He received some basic training at Camp Roberts, was transferred to Jefferson Barracks for more training and then sent to the Paducah area for guard duty in early 1862. He fought in the Battle of Shiloh and was shot in the left knee on the first day (Sunday, April 6, 1862). He was sent by hospital steamboat to a military hospital in Cincinnati, but died May 12, 1862. The Civil War clearly took a toll on the Hamilton County Allen family.

William's son and my grandfather, Howard Anderson Allen, was born on July 4, 1861 probably on the family farm in the area near Ten Mile Church in Hamilton County. This raises another imponderable question: why would his father enlist in the Union Army in October 1861 despite the fact that he had a newborn son and he was 37 years old, an age now considered too old for military service? Howard married Laura Marsh in 1891. They had six children, Nella, Rella, Omar, Lorraine and two children who died in infancy. At some time during this marriage, they moved from the family farm near Ten Mile Church to a small farm located approximately three miles east of Dahlgren. Omar Allen was my father, and this is this as far as I will take the history of the Josiah Allen family.

---

the Raid had anything to do with the campaign against Vicksburg.

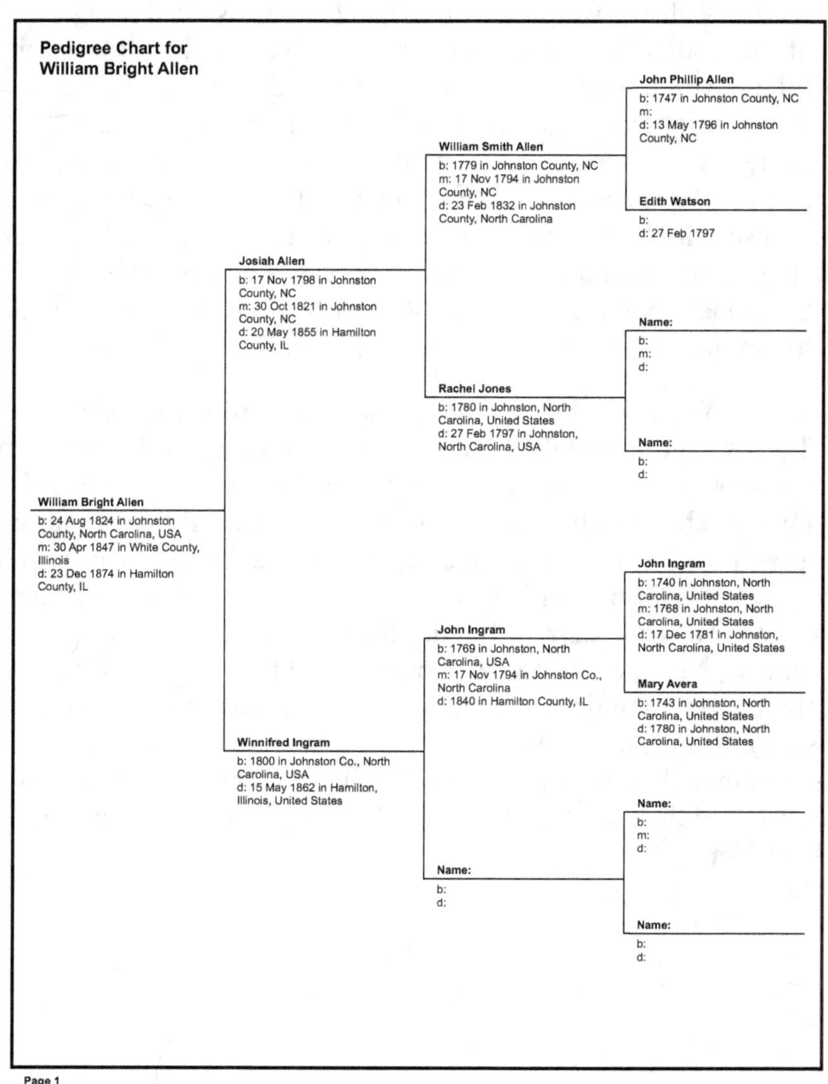

Pedigree Chart for
William Bright Allen

John Phillip Allen
b: 1747 in Johnston County, NC
m:
d: 13 May 1796 in Johnston County, NC

William Smith Allen
b: 1779 in Johnston County, NC
m: 17 Nov 1794 in Johnston County, NC
d: 23 Feb 1832 in Johnston County, North Carolina

Edith Watson
b:
d: 27 Feb 1797

Josiah Allen
b: 17 Nov 1798 in Johnston County, NC
m: 30 Oct 1821 in Johnston County, NC
d: 20 May 1855 in Hamilton County, IL

Name:
b:
m:
d:

Rachel Jones
b: 1780 in Johnston, North Carolina, United States
d: 27 Feb 1797 in Johnston, North Carolina, USA

Name:
b:
d:

William Bright Allen
b: 24 Aug 1824 in Johnston County, North Carolina, USA
m: 30 Apr 1847 in White County, Illinois
d: 23 Dec 1874 in Hamilton County, IL

John Ingram
b: 1740 in Johnston, North Carolina, United States
m: 1768 in Johnston, North Carolina, United States
d: 17 Dec 1781 in Johnston, North Carolina, United States

John Ingram
b: 1769 in Johnston, North Carolina, USA
m: 17 Nov 1794 in Johnston Co., North Carolina
d: 1840 in Hamilton County, IL

Mary Avera
b: 1743 in Johnston, North Carolina, United States
d: 1780 in Johnston, North Carolina, United States

Winnifred Ingram
b: 1800 in Johnston Co., North Carolina, USA
d: 15 May 1862 in Hamilton, Illinois, United States

Name:
b:
m:
d:

Name:
b:
d:

Name:
b:
d:

William Bright Allen

Howard Henderson Allen and Laura Marsh Allen

CHAPTER 3

THE JOHN INGRAM FAMILY

It appears that the first of John Ingram's North American ancestors was Richard Ingram who was probably born in North Carolina sometime around 1715 and died in Johnston County, North Carolina in 1780.

John Ingram (1769-1840) was born in Johnston County, North Carolina in 1769. He married Catherine Sewell (1775-1823) in 1799, and they had at least ten children. I know very little about her family; her father's name was John Sewell, but I have unearthed almost no information about him.

I do not at present have much information about this family, but probably their oldest son, Sewell was born in Johnston County in 1809 and most of the rest the family was born in Johnston County. One child, however, Penelope Ingram, was born in McNairy County, Tennessee in 1823. In that same year, 1823, Catherine Ingram died in McNairy County, almost certainly in childbirth.

CHAPTER 4

THE THOMAS MARSH FAMILY

The first member of this family for whom I have any information is John Marsh (1730-1807) who was born in Surrey County, North Carolina in 1730 (this information was obtained on Ancestry.com from other researchers and is not confirmed). I have a copy of his will dated October 13, 1807. It is useful in providing the names of his surviving children. To his wife, Mary, he left most of his property amounting to 100 acres along with four horses, "a feather bead [sic] and two cows and seven head of hogs and my household furniture." No slaves were mentioned. He signed the will with an X indicating, of course, that he was illiterate like so many of the small farmers in Appalachia in the 17th century.[12]

One of his sons, Thomas Marsh (1766-1840), was born in Surrey County, North Carolina and died in Warren County, Tennessee in 1840. Nothing is known about when Thomas migrated to Tennessee or by what way he arrived. Probably there was not much for him in North Carolina – – in his father's will he was remembered with 15 shillings (in 2022 approximately $60.00)! His son, William B. Marsh (1797-1867), was born in Surrey County, North Carolina where he married Edith Paul (1797-1870) on October 15, 1817. They, and probably Williams B.'s father and other members of the family, moved to Bledsoe County, Tennessee in 1817.

One of William B.'s sons and my great grandfather, Thomas Marsh (1828-1912), was born in Warren County,

---

[12] North Carolina, Wills and Probate Records,1665-1998 for John Marsh. Ancestry.com.

Tennessee in March, 1828.[13] Thomas married Nancy Ann Moss on June 6, 1850 in Bledsoe County when Nancy was only 15 years old. They moved to Hamilton County, Illinois soon after their marriage and the first of three children was born in Hamilton County in 1854. Nancy died in 1858, the same year her third child was born. Two years later, according to the 1860 census, Thomas was unmarried and living with his three children, another nine-year-old child and two teenagers, an 18-year-old male, who is listed as a farm laborer, and a 16-year-old girl.

Several other members of the William B. Marsh family moved from Tennessee, probably at the same time Thomas moved to Hamilton County and settled in Laclede County, Missouri. Thomas's brother William lived through the Civil War years in Missouri, but in February,1865 William enlisted as a Corporal in Company H, 155th Illinois Infantry in Ashley, Illinois. The war ended in April 1865 so it was only a short term of service for William. The federal enlistment bonus may have played a part in this act of patriotism. William moved to Hamilton County after his discharge from military service.[14]

Two years after Thomas's wife Nancy's death on June 19, 1860 he married Charlotta Morgan (1838-1920). Charlotta was born in Polk County, Illinois February 22, 1838. Her father was Uriah James Morgan, born in Virginia in 1798 and died in Adams County, Illinois in 1840. Her mother was Rachel Robinson, who was born in Kentucky in 1798 and died in Hamilton County, Illinois in 1899. She is buried next to Thomas and Charlotta Morgan Marsh in Richardson Hill Cemetery near Dahlgren, Illinois. Charlotta married Hardy Damon in 1858; they had one

———————————————————

[13]Sources differ on his place of birth. One records his birth in Bledsoe County, but his Certificate of Disability for Discharge from the Union Army reported his birth was in Warren County, Tennessee.

[14] Illinois, Database of Illinois Veterans Index, 1775-1995.

daughter, Jerusha, before Damon died in 1859. Thomas and Charlotta had six children together, and one of them, Laura Marsh, would marry Howard Henderson Allen and become my grandmother.[15]

Thomas joined many of his neighbors along with the Allens and the Ingrams to enlist in Company D, 6th Illinois Cavalry in McLeansboro as a Sergeant for three years on October 11, 1861. His enlistment papers record that he was 31 years old, 6 foot one with a fair complexion and dark eyes. This was, of course, the same company in which my great-grandfather William Bright Allen also served as Quartermaster Sergeant. Thomas served until November 13, 1862 when he was discharged for medical reasons at a hospital in Memphis, Tennessee. According to his discharge certificate, he was sick with typhoid fever in Paducah, Kentucky in March 1862 and since then suffering from "climate & rough camp life." Elsewhere in his application for pension in 1886, Thomas recorded that he suffered as well from "rupture of left side on the March from Columbus, Ky to Trenton, Tennessee in June 1862 and disease of the breast and spermatic cord at Memphis Tennessee, in October 1862."

Toward the end the war, on March 4, 1865, Thomas enlisted in Company I, 58th Illinois Infantry and was discharged May 29, 1865-- only three months service. I have found little information about this experience, but my guess is that Thomas, like his brother William, enlisted for a bonus that was available at that time. The 58th Illinois infantry was involved in many of General Ulysses S. Grant's campaigns including fighting at Fort Donelson, Fort Henry and the siege of Vicksburg among other

---

[15] Pension record of Thomas Marsh, General Index to Pension Files, 1861-1934 (National Archives). A roster of the names of the members of Co. D, 6th Illinois Volunteer Cavalry probably at the time of organization of the unit is in Carol Lee Yarbrough, "The Yesterdays of Hamilton County, Illinois.carolyar.com/Illinois/Hamilton County.htm.

campaigns, but of course Thomas was not involved in any of this.

Unlike many Union Army veterans, Thomas March lived a long and prosperous life after the war and died December 28, 1912. He was buried at Richardson Hill Cemetery where his wife Charlotta was buried next to him in 1920.

Thomas Marsh, c.1910

Thomas and Charlotta Morgan Marsh

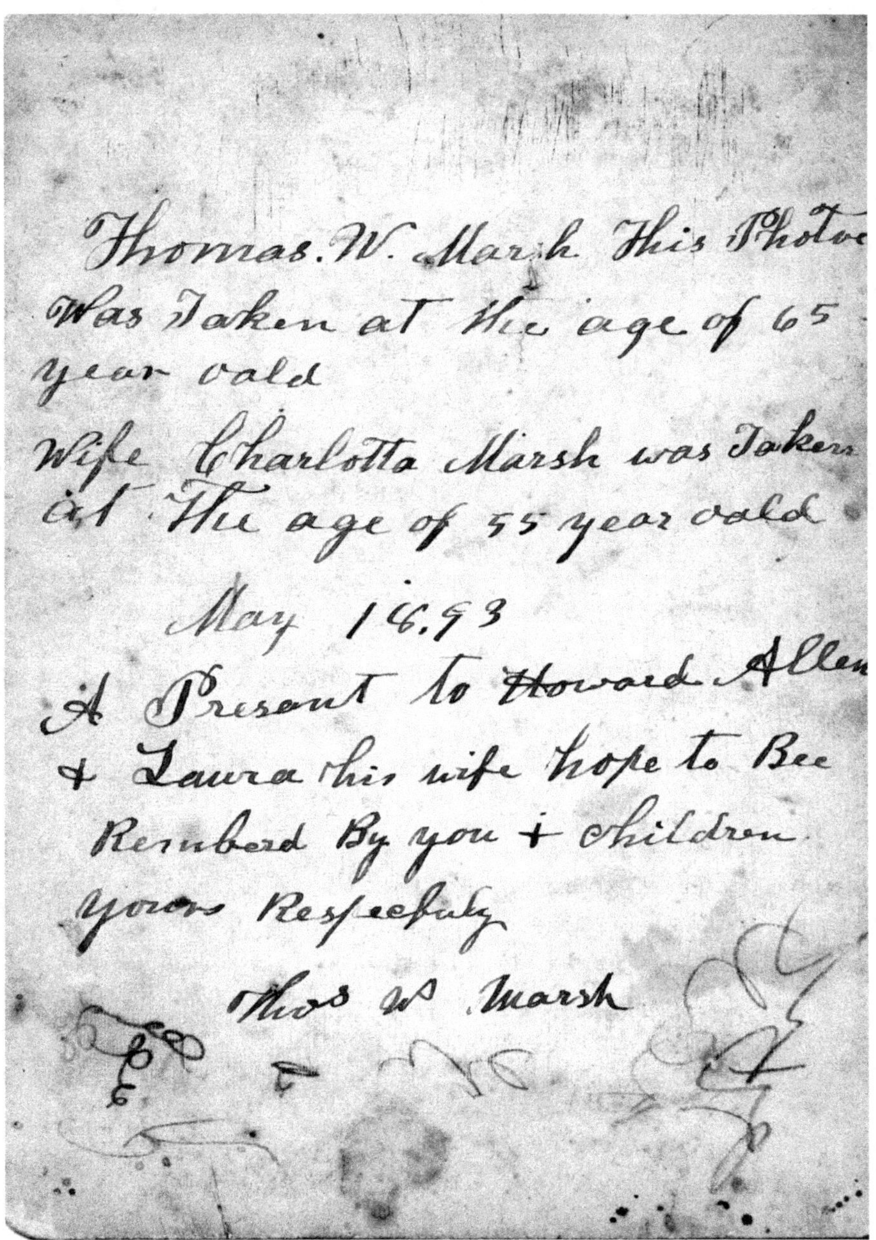

This note was written on the back of the preceding photograph of
Thomas and Charlotta Marsh.

The Marsh Family Reunion, c. 1905

Standing (left to right): Thomas Marsh, Charlotta Morgan Marsh, James M. Marsh (standing in front of his grandparents) Robert Allen (Howard's brother), Howard Allen, Laura Allen (Howard Allen's wife and daughter of Thomas and Charlotta Marsh), Dr. Sam Allen (son of Joe Allen, a physician in Robinson, Illinois), Unknown, Clara Goin Rhodes (daughter of Rado DeWitt Goin), Jasper Goin (son of Rado DeWitt Goin), Rado DeWitt Goin (Howard Allen's first cousin), Unknown (perhaps a daughter of Thomas and Charlotta Marsh), and probably Jurusha Damon Compton, (Charlotta Marsh's daughter from her first marriage).

Seated: Mrs. J. H. Hart, J. H. Hart, Dora Hart Allen (daughter of J.H. Hart and wife of William Allen), William "Bill" Allen (son of Joe and Louise Allen); owned a grocery store in Dahlgren), Louise Allen (wife of Joe Allen), Joe Allen (brother of Howard and Robert Allen and an undertaker in Dahlgren).

Seated on the grass from left to right: children of Howard and Laura Allen (Effa, Omar, Rella and Nella), Bertha Allen (daughter of Joe and Louisa Allen), Unknown, Unknown.

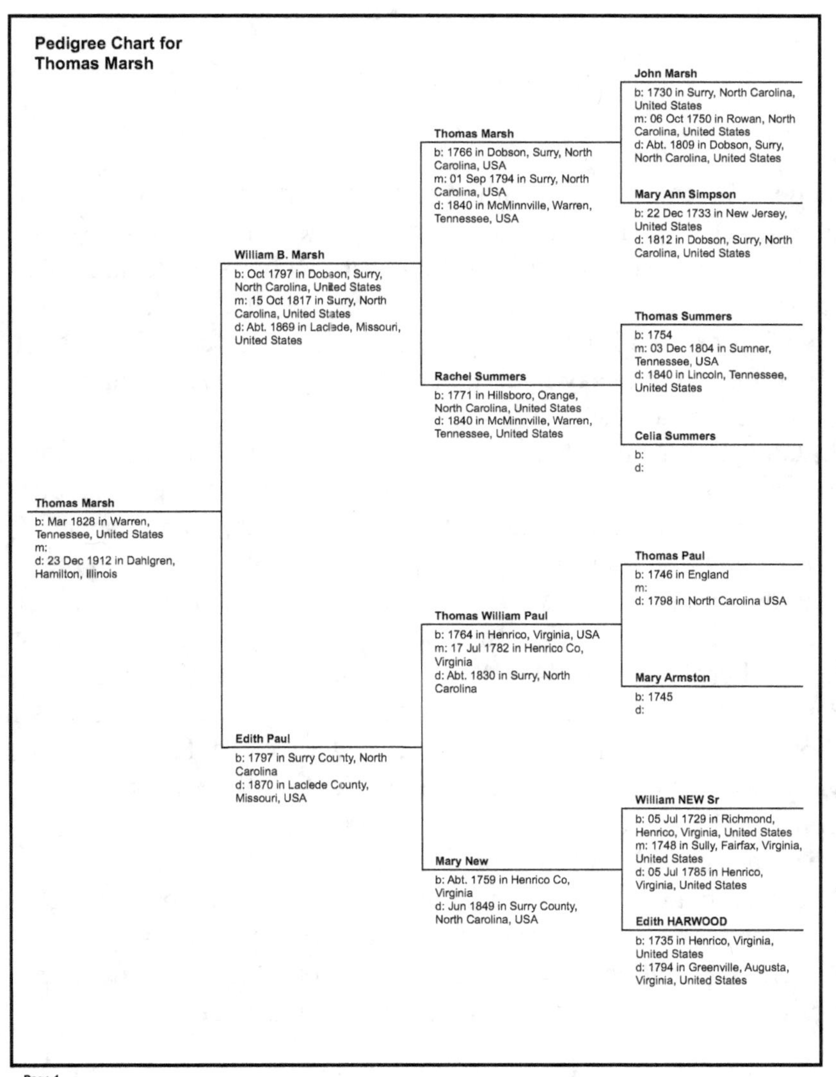

Pedigree Chart for
Thomas Marsh

Thomas Marsh
b: Mar 1828 in Warren, Tennessee, United States
m:
d: 23 Dec 1912 in Dahlgren, Hamilton, Illinois

William B. Marsh
b: Oct 1797 in Dobson, Surry, North Carolina, United States
m: 15 Oct 1817 in Surry, North Carolina, United States
d: Abt. 1869 in Laclede, Missouri, United States

Edith Paul
b: 1797 in Surry County, North Carolina
d: 1870 in Laclede County, Missouri, USA

Thomas Marsh
b: 1766 in Dobson, Surry, North Carolina, USA
m: 01 Sep 1794 in Surry, North Carolina, USA
d: 1840 in McMinnville, Warren, Tennessee, USA

Rachel Summers
b: 1771 in Hillsboro, Orange, North Carolina, United States
d: 1840 in McMinnville, Warren, Tennessee, United States

Thomas William Paul
b: 1764 in Henrico, Virginia, USA
m: 17 Jul 1782 in Henrico Co, Virginia
d: Abt. 1830 in Surry, North Carolina

Mary New
b: Abt. 1759 in Henrico Co, Virginia
d: Jun 1849 in Surry County, North Carolina, USA

John Marsh
b: 1730 in Surry, North Carolina, United States
m: 06 Oct 1750 in Rowan, North Carolina, United States
d: Abt. 1809 in Dobson, Surry, North Carolina, United States

Mary Ann Simpson
b: 22 Dec 1733 in New Jersey, United States
d: 1812 in Dobson, Surry, North Carolina, United States

Thomas Summers
b: 1754
m: 03 Dec 1804 in Sumner, Tennessee, USA
d: 1840 in Lincoln, Tennessee, United States

Celia Summers
b:
d:

Thomas Paul
b: 1746 in England
m:
d: 1798 in North Carolina USA

Mary Armston
b: 1745
d:

William NEW Sr
b: 05 Jul 1729 in Richmond, Henrico, Virginia, United States
m: 1748 in Sully, Fairfax, Virginia, United States
d: 05 Jul 1785 in Henrico, Virginia, United States

Edith HARWOOD
b: 1735 in Henrico, Virginia, United States
d: 1794 in Greenville, Augusta, Virginia, United States

CHAPTER 5

THE LEWIS WILSON FAMILY

I am not as comfortable with my findings about the history of the ancestors of Lewis Wilson as I am with the Allen family history, mainly because of the work of Merritt E. Roberts on Josiah Allen's family, and there are probably some errors in the Wilson genealogy which I have compiled from Ancestry.com. Even so, I am comfortable in saying that probably my first Wilson ancestor in North America, Joseph Wilson (1714-1794), arrived in Philadelphia from Ireland sometime early in the 18th-century; a Joseph Wilson is listed on a ship manifest in Philadelphia dated 1739. He was born in Ireland in 1714, and he apparently spent most of his life after his arrival in the American colonies in the Philadelphia area. His will was probated, and he was buried in or very near Harrisburg, Dauphin County, Pennsylvania. His oldest son, Robert Wilson (1741-1817), born in Dauphin County, Pennsylvania in 1741, was married in that county to Ester Parks in 1760. He enlisted in 1776 in the Lancaster County Revolutionary Militia (8th Company, 6th Battalion in Captain Ramsey's Company). Sometime after that Robert Wilson migrated west to the area around Fort Pitt (Pittsburgh) in Indiana County, Pennsylvania and he died in that county in 1817. Apparently, a large number of members of the Wilson clan, perhaps related to Robert, also settled in that same area surrounding Fort Pitt when western Pennsylvania was a very rough, isolated frontier.

One of Robert Wilson's sons, Lewis Wilson, my great-great-great grandfather, was born in Westmoreland County also near Fort Pitt. In 1800 Lewis was recorded as a resident of Butler County, Pennsylvania which is to the northwest of Indiana County near the Allegheny River just north of Fort Pitt. A history of the Wilson family in New Harmony, Indiana by Dolores E. March covers Lewis Wilson's family only very briefly, but she does indicate that a Lewis Wilson owned some 400 acres of land in

Butler County and that he served on a grand jury in 1804.[16] Or, perhaps March discovered another Lewis Wilson, for it seems unlikely that he would have abandoned a 400-acre Pennsylvania farm. But despite any property he may have owned in Butler County, Pennsylvania, soon after 1804 Lewis Wilson moved to a frontier community on the Wabash River originally called "Harmony" in what is now the state of Indiana.

The Harmony community on the Wabash River was founded by George Rapp, a minister and the leader of a congregation of approximately 300 people from Württemberg, Germany, a small group of religious zealots who shared George Rapp's belief that Western civilization was lost in sin and the only solution was to withdraw entirely from Western society. Rapp and his followers tried several locations in North America before they settled temporarily in 1804 in Butler County, Pennsylvania where the group created a community that they called "Harmony." Apparently, even Butler County was too "civilized" for the Rappites, and, seeking greater isolation, they moved down the Ohio River to a location on the Wabash River in what is now Posey County, Indiana that the Rappites also called "Harmony."[17]

Probably Lewis Wilson became acquainted with George Rapp during Rapp's brief sojourn in Butler County, and he moved to Harmony, Indiana at the same time that the Rapp community moved or soon thereafter. I'm sure of this because I have a manuscript dated December 29, 1815 from a Caleb Mathew to Frederick Rapp: "Emigration from Butler County to the Wabash; decline of the Old Harmony." Apparently, Mathew had recently just returned from the Harmony settlement on the Wabash and was acting in Butler County as a business representative for George Rapp. He wrote that a Robert Wilson expressed an intention to "move Down in the spring" and that an Alexander Wilson "will

---

[16] Dolores Eckroat March, "In Retrospect Wilson" (1998, updated 2006). A copy of the typed manuscript is in my possession.

[17] History of Butler County, Pennsylvania (R. G. Brown & Co., Chicago, 1895)

move Down in the spring if he can sel [sic] his land."[18]

But the most relevant point to my essay is that Mathew also informed Frederick Rapp in a separate note on October 22, 1818 that "Mr. Louis [sic] Wilson leaves this place for Homonie tomorrow morning & takes the horse purchased of A. Ziegler with him and will be the bearer of this letter. Agreeable to the advice of Ziegler we have instructed Mr. Wilson to travel slow not more than 20 miles a day for a week and then he may increase to 25 & 30 but not more. The horse has not been used to traveling has always in stood in the stable, and that if he should be pushed on the road he might be killed or materially injured."[19]

It should be emphasized that travel in this part of North America around the beginning of the 19th century was not what most of us today would consider attempting. The dangers and uncertainties must have been comparable to the dangers of ocean travel between Great Britain and North America. Conditions of travel of families downstream on the Ohio River from the Pittsburgh area to any area in the Ohio River Valley mostly by flat boat, as was the case on the Tennessee River in the same years, was dangerous and unpredictable. In the 1780s the first settlements were established in the Ohio territory. Fear of hostile Native Americans continued to be a major obstacle to the western movement into the Ohio Valley until after the Battle of Fallen Timbers in 1794 effectively ended the Native American threat, although small bands of Native Americans remained in the area for

---

[18] <u>History of the Decedents of Lewis Wilson</u> (Compiled by Judge Herdis P. Clements for the Wilson Reunion – August 1, 1937 Held at New Harmony, Indiana.) Robert Wilson, Lewis Wilson's father died in in 1817 in Blairsville, Indiana—about 12 miles from New Harmony. "The Wilsons of Posey County, Indiana and Allied Families," compiled by John Wm. Epley, February 10, 1999. Revised and corrected, May 8, 1999.

[19] Ibid.

many years thereafter.[20]

Lewis Wilson is listed as a resident of Posey County, in the 1840 United States Census. He apparently lived there until he died in 1850. With the arrival of others who were not affiliated with the Rapp Community, the Rappites apparently failed to find the isolation from society that they sought in Harmony so in 1825 George Rapp sold his holdings in Indiana to Robert Dale Owen from Great Britain who named the settlement New Harmony and so it has been ever since. Owen had his own visionary plan to create a new communitarian society in the wilderness without the pietism of George Rapp, but Owen, too, failed and he returned to Britain in 1828. He left the property in New Harmony in the hands of his eight children who, with the scientists, teachers and intellectuals who he had recruited to the area, remained in New Harmony to develop "one of the most notable pre-Civil War cultural centers in the United States."[21] New Harmony was a striking contrast with the remainder of this part of southern Indiana that was settled primarily by small farmers from the South.

Lewis Wilson was married to Mary Moore (1773-1832) in 1794. I can find almost no information about Mary Moore (1773-1832) except that she was born in Pennsylvania in 1773. They had eight children according to my records; the first was born in 1794, and the last in 1808. All his children were born in Butler County, Pennsylvania so it is pretty clear that the migration from Butler County to Posey County, Indiana did not take place until after 1808.

One of the children of Lewis and Mary Wilson was David Wilson (my direct ancestor) who was born in Butler County,

---

[20] D. McCullough, <u>The Pioneers</u>, 43-118.

[21] "New Harmony," <u>Encyclopedia Britannica</u> (Revised and updated by Amy Tikkanen 2020) https: www.britannica.com/place/New Harmony.

Pennsylvania in 1800. David moved with his family to Posey County, Indiana; and he spent the rest of his life as a farmer in that county until he died in 1875. He married Sabrina Stallings in 1822, and my records show that they had six children, one of them my great-grandfather, Isaac Wilson (1834-1906).

Sabrina Stallings's father was Wright Stallings who was born in Franklin County, North Carolina in 1750 and died in Posey County in 1828. If the records I have found about Wright are correct, he had at least two wives and over ten children. I have the dates of the birth of the children ranging from 1782 to 1803 when Sabrina, his last child, was born. According to the Census of 1820 Wright owned two slaves, one a male over 45 years old and a female between ages 14-25 despite slavery being illegal in Indiana. Wright Stallings died in Posey County in 1828. In his Memoirs my grandfather Robert Wilson recorded that the Stallings family "brought a number of slaves with them from North Carolina. These, of course, became free when their owners brought them north of the Ohio river. I've often heard my father speak of these old Negroes who continued to live along with their previous owners. One old man Grandpa especially remembered was named Hawk. He taught my father to play many of the old-time fiddle tunes he knew."[22]

Isaac Wilson, my great-grandfather, was born in Posey County in 1834. In the manuscript census of 1850, he is recorded living with his father and mother in Posey County as a farmer. In 1860 the manuscript census records him as living with another family as a farm laborer. Isaac's life would change dramatically in 1861 with the beginning of the Civil War. The war broke out in April 1861, and Isaac Wilson enlisted in Posey County on November 15, 1861 for three years as a Sgt. in Company C, 60th Indiana Volunteer Infantry.

---

[22] "The Memoirs of Robert Wilson," Appendix 1, 10.

The 60th Regiment was organized in Evansville and Indianapolis, and for a short time was stationed in Indianapolis guarding prisoners. From there it was transferred to Kentucky to serve as a unit in the Union Army that was involved in campaigns under General Ulysses S. Grant and General William Tecumseh Sherman focused mainly on the Mississippi and Tennessee rivers. It was involved in Grant's siege of Vicksburg, Mississippi and in the campaign against Jackson, Mississippi which was part of the overall Grant strategy in the victory at Vicksburg. The 60th Indiana infantry closed out the war and was discharged in Thibodeaux, Louisiana.[23]

I have no record to show that Isaac Wilson was personally involved in any fighting, but the 60th Indiana Infantry was involved in considerable action. He was promoted to 1st Sgt. on February 18, 1863, a rank which was vacated by Alexander Stallings, Isaac Wilson's first cousin, who probably enlisted at the same time Isaac Wilson enlisted, along with Luther Wilson, Isaac's brother. Stallings was promoted to 1st Lieutenant in Company C. in 1864, and when Stallings was promoted to Captain, Isaac Wilson was promoted to 1st Lt. This is a record which indicates that Isaac had been very successful in meeting his responsibilities as an infantry officer whatever they may have been, so he was probably involved in at least some combat.[24]

One additional item of interest is that Isaac's younger brother, Luther, who enlisted at the same time as Isaac in Company C, 60th Indiana Volunteer Infantry, along with their cousin Alexander Stallings. In November 1863 Cpl. Luther Wilson was reported captured by the Confederate Army. In January,1864 Luther was paroled by the Confederates and was quartered by the Union army in a "parole camp" near New Orleans, Louisiana.

---

[23] 60th Regimental Infantry (3 Years' Service); (Report of the Adjutant General of the State of Indiana,1865)

[24] Service Record of Isaac Wilson, Co. C, 60th Indiana Infantry, CMSR.

Luther apparently had had enough of the war, so he left his assignment and returned to Posey County. He was arrested, charged with desertion and transported to Cairo, Illinois and then back to his company which was stationed at the time in Carrollton, Louisiana. He was court-martialed and found guilty by his superior officers, Capt. Stallings (his first cousin) and his brother, Lt. Isaac Wilson. Luther lost his rank and was apparently fined, $40.39 and returned to duty. A rather lenient sentence for desertion when many Civil War deserters were executed for similar offenses![25]

Lt. Isaac Wilson was discharged from the Union army when his Company was mustered out of the service in Indianapolis, Indiana on March 2, 1865. The manuscript Census of 1870 found him working as a farm laborer with a family in Posey County. My next record of Isaac locates him in Shawneetown, Gallatin County, Illinois where he married Martha Ann Crunk (1849-1925 in November, 1871. They settled on a farm in White County, Illinois just a couple of miles west of Texas City.[26]

Martha Crunk, or "Patsy," as she was commonly called, was born in Posey County, Indiana on April 2, 1849. Her father, David Smith Crunk, was also born in Posey County in 1824, but his father John G. Crunk was born in North Carolina in 1775 and died in Posey County in 1844. Probably his first ancestor in North America was a Nathaniel Crunk who was born in Virginia in 1675 and died in North Carolina in 1767. In his Memoirs Robert Wilson recalls that his mother's father "was a singing teacher of the old school. He taught note reading in the old Southern Harmony

---

[25] Service Record of Luther Wilson, Co. C. 60th Indiana Infantry. CMSR.

[26] Pension record of Isaac Wilson, General Index to Pension Files, 1861-1934 (National Archives).

system oval-shaped notes and conducted singing classes."[27]

Robert remembered his mother as having "a really fine singing voice, and while I have no means of knowing for sure, it is my opinion that few women anywhere or anytime could reach higher notes than she could. Her voice was sweet and very reasonable yet very strong and powerful. Many times, I remember near sundown she would be caring for the milk cows and calves at the bars in the Front Lot and invariably singing some of the many songs she knew by heart. She would sing from memory every line of scores of old-time songs – – folksongs, religious songs almost any kind." Clearly this was a family which had inherited a great love and talent for music, and I should also point out that Isaac Wilson was also a talented musician, for Grandpa Wilson points out in his Memoirs that his father occasionally played fiddle for square dances for the local community.

Robert also writes in his Memoirs about a very unpleasant confrontation with his father. He remembered that his father was especially careful in cultivating some plum sprouts with the idea of producing fresh fruit for the family table. Robert, then only a very small boy, in play attacked the plum sprouts with his mother's butcher knife. His father apparently reacted in rage, but Robert is very sketchy about what happened next. My mother related to me the same story on more than one occasion, but in her version, which apparently, she heard from her father, Robert's father nearly beat him to death. His back was so severely injured in the beating that for years he was unable to work in the fields with the men and spent a great deal more time than would ordinarily have been the case with his mother. In fact, I remember that Grandpa Wilson always walked with a very awkward, stiff back. My mother said it was in these years when he was convalescing my grandfather learned the folk songs from his mother that were later recorded and deposited in the National Archives.

---

[27] Robert Wilson, Memoirs, Appendix I.

Robert Wilson (1876-1957) was born on his family's farm near Texas City in 1876. His first marriage was to Hattie Wilson in 1897. They had three children, Ruby, Sumner, and Edith. Hattie died in 1904. I have very little information about Hattie. She was born in Illinois, and her last name was Wilson so perhaps she may have been distantly related to Robert. There was a fairly large Wilson clan in Posey County, and back in Butler County, Pennsylvania. Her family may have been one of the Wilson families who moved into southern Indiana at about the same time that Isaac Wilson and his brother Luther made the same move. According to the 1900 manuscript census her parents were both born in Tennessee, not Pennsylvania, and of course not all people with the last name Wilson are related.

Robert Wilson married Edith Brinkley (1880-1962) my grandmother, in 1906. Edith was previously married to Serenius Sigler in 1900 in Hamilton County, and they had one son, Vernon Sigler, who grew to adulthood. Serenius died in 1905 and Edith married Robert Wilson the next year.

The Isaac Wilson Family, c. 1900

Front row, left to right: Sam Gaines (husband of Delia Wilson), Fred Wilson, Robert Wilson (holding infants Ruby and Sumner Wilson), unknown infant, Allie Wilson, Arthur Wilson (standing), Isaac Wilson.

Standing left to right: Dela Wilson Gaines, Mary Wilson, a neighbor, Hattie Wilson (Robert's wife) holding Edith Wilson) Minnie Gaines Wilson (Allie Wilson's wife and infant), and Martha Crunk Wilson (Isaac's wife).

Martha Crunk Wilson, c. 1920

Robert and Edith Wilson, c. 1910

CHAPTER 6

THE WILLIAM BRINKLEY FAMILY

Edith Brinkley's father was Robert Ewing Brinkley (1856-1906). He was born in Gallatin County, Illinois in 1856. He married Martha Ann Hall (1860-1931) in 1879, and they continued to live in Gallatin County until approximately 1890 when they appear in the 1890 census as residents of Hamilton County. They had several children, but I think only three grew to adulthood: Ruth, Edith and Susan. (I remember her fondly as my "Aunt Susie"; we spent a lot of holidays at her magnificent house in McLeansboro.)

This branch of the Brinkley family can be traced with limited confidence to Jacob Brinkley who was born in England and died in Virginia in 1685. His son, also named Peter, was born in Virginia around 1700 and died in Perquimans County, North Carolina in the 1770s. Some descendants of this family remained in North Carolina for three generations until William Brinkley moved with his family to Tennessee and then on to Gallatin County, Illinois around 1830. His son, William Brinkley, was born in Tennessee, but was with his family in Gallatin by about 1830. Records indicate that he married Mary Greer in 1831 and that he was appointed United States Postmaster for McLeansboro in 1851. He lived in Hamilton County until his death in 1873.

William Brinkley's son John Brinkley (1836-1870) was born in Gallatin County, Illinois in 1836, and he married Francis E. Crawford in 1853 in Gallatin County where they lived most of their lives. During the Civil War John enlisted in Company K of the 131st Illinois infantry regiment in 1862, but his experiences in the early days of that regiment were unfortunate to say the least. The regiment was recruited primarily from the counties of southern Illinois and was stationed originally at Fort Massac with approximately 815 enlisted men plus officers. Unfortunately, they were mustered at Fort Massac "without tents, camp equipage or guns, except a few inferior guns borrowed for use in guard duty and squad drill." Measles broke out in the camp quickly, and approximately 100 of the men were stricken, most died or were discharged for disability. The regiment went on to serve in major campaigns in the Mississippi river area, but at this point I have no further record of Private Brinkley's service.[28] He died in Gallatin County in 1870.

John Brinkley married Francis E. Crawford (1836-1870) in Gallatin County in 1853. Her Crawford ancestors can be traced back to a John Crawford who was born in Ireland about 1760 and died in Gallatin County, Illinois in 1833. Their grandson and my great grandfather, Robert Ewing Brinkley (1856-1906) was born in Gallatin County in 1856. Both of his parents died in 1870, and in the 1870 manuscript census Robert, 13 years old, and his sister, Mary, 15 years old, are registered as residents in the household of a William Davis, apparently unrelated. Informal adoption of this kind of orphaned children was fairly common in the 19th century as study of the manuscript census graphically reveals.

Robert Brinkley married Martha Ann Hall in 1879 in Gallatin County. They had at least three children who survived infancy, and one of them, Edith Brinkley, would become my grandmother. Martha Hall's ancestors in North America can be traced back to Henry Hall, born in England about 1715 and died in Georgia in 1799. The first of his descendants to arrive in southern Illinois was his grandson Alfred Hall (1800-1835) who is recorded

---

[28] Adjutant General's Report, "131 Illinois Infantry Regiment History," ILGenWeb Project. John Brinkley's brother, George W. Brinkley enlisted in Company D. 6th Illinois Cavalry when it was organized in McLeansboro in 1861, and he probably participated in Griersons Raid. He was killed after the Raid in July, 1863. https://www.fold3.com/image/293015390?terms=civil,brinkley,us, george,war&xid=1945

as having married Jane Robinson (1804-1855) in White County, Illinois in 1818. He died in Wayne County in 1835. His son Henry Hall (1822-1863) married Mary Jane Moore (1830-1910) in Wayne County in 1846. Henry Hall died in the Union Army General Hospital in 1863 at Mound City, Illinois as a Private in the 16th Illinois Infantry. Unfortunately, I have no additional information about his military service, but my son Mark (1962-) and I did locate his gravesite at the National Cemetery in Mounds, Illinois in August 2021.

The Robert Brinkley Family

Seated from left to right: Ruth Brinkley, Martha Hall Brinkley, Robert Brinkley, Mary Hall Moore Smith, Ella Brinkley

Standing: Edith Brinkley, Susan Jane Brinkley

William Brinkley

Serenius and Edith Brinkley Sigler

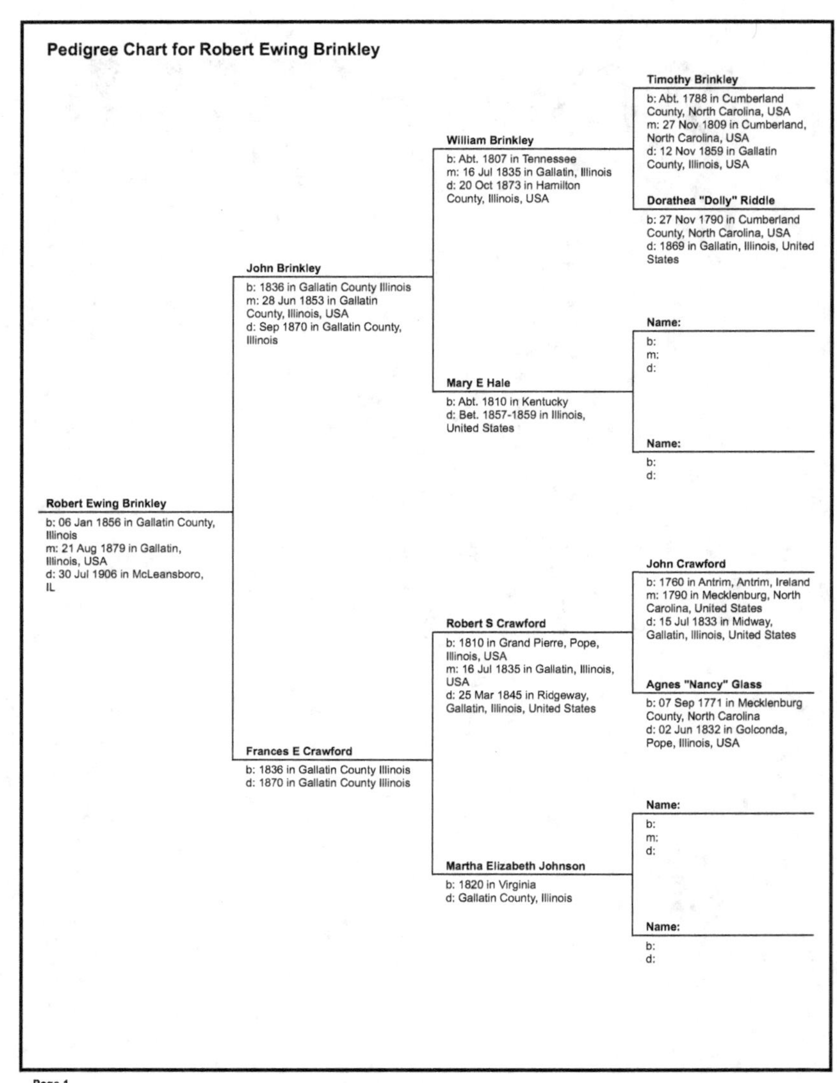

Pedigree Chart for Robert Ewing Brinkley

Timothy Brinkley
b: Abt. 1788 in Cumberland County, North Carolina, USA
m: 27 Nov 1809 in Cumberland, North Carolina, USA
d: 12 Nov 1859 in Gallatin County, Illinois, USA

William Brinkley
b: Abt. 1807 in Tennessee
m: 16 Jul 1835 in Gallatin, Illinois
d: 20 Oct 1873 in Hamilton County, Illinois, USA

Dorathea "Dolly" Riddle
b: 27 Nov 1790 in Cumberland County, North Carolina, USA
d: 1869 in Gallatin, Illinois, United States

John Brinkley
b: 1836 in Gallatin County Illinois
m: 28 Jun 1853 in Gallatin County, Illinois, USA
d: Sep 1870 in Gallatin County, Illinois

Name:
b:
m:
d:

Mary E Hale
b: Abt. 1810 in Kentucky
d: Bet. 1857-1859 in Illinois, United States

Name:
b:
d:

Robert Ewing Brinkley
b: 06 Jan 1856 in Gallatin County, Illinois
m: 21 Aug 1879 in Gallatin, Illinois, USA
d: 30 Jul 1906 in McLeansboro, IL

John Crawford
b: 1760 in Antrim, Antrim, Ireland
m: 1790 in Mecklenburg, North Carolina, United States
d: 15 Jul 1833 in Midway, Gallatin, Illinois, United States

Robert S Crawford
b: 1810 in Grand Pierre, Pope, Illinois, USA
m: 16 Jul 1835 in Gallatin, Illinois, USA
d: 25 Mar 1845 in Ridgeway, Gallatin, Illinois, United States

Agnes "Nancy" Glass
b: 07 Sep 1771 in Mecklenburg County, North Carolina
d: 02 Jun 1832 in Golconda, Pope, Illinois, USA

Frances E Crawford
b: 1836 in Gallatin County Illinois
d: 1870 in Gallatin County Illinois

Name:
b:
m:
d:

Martha Elizabeth Johnson
b: 1820 in Virginia
d: Gallatin County, Illinois

Name:
b:
d:

Page 1

CHAPTER 7

OMAR "PETIE" ALLEN

Omar Ethan "Petie" Allen (1902-1986), my father, was born on a small farm east of Dahlgren in 1902. He was the only surviving son of Howard and Laura Allen; two children died in infancy and are buried in Richardson Hill Cemetery. He had four surviving sisters, Effa (1892-1928), Nella (1893-1988), Rella (1896-1985), and Lorraine (1906-1991). I remember his sisters always accused him of being spoiled by his mother, and my experience would confirm that.

Not long after he was born, his father, Howard Henderson Allen, retired from farming and moved his family to Dahlgren where Dad would live the rest of his life. I don't know much about his early days, but I do know that he played on the Dahlgren High School basketball team although he never graduated from high school. Sometime in the early 1920s he and his sister Nell entered a partnership to open a restaurant in Dahlgren which was always known as Allen's Café.

The 1920s were apparently good times in Dahlgren, and their enterprise was very successful. It was located in a building in downtown Dahlgren, and it offered an ice cream parlor, two pool tables, and in the 1920s apparently a fairly ambitious menu. It had a soda fountain, and Dad's mother made pies daily for several years. He talked quite a lot about those days, and most of his stories I have forgotten. But I do recall tales about fast cars, burned out engines and a good deal of alcoholic consumption. It is fair to conclude that he was a rounder, and times were very good. Then in 1929 the stock market collapsed and the Dahlgren economy sank with it, not ever to recover. Of course, he did not know it at the time, but it was the end of small-town vitality and economic prosperity in the United States.

Sometime in the early years of the Depression Dad met my mother, Helen Marie Wilson (1907-2009), and they were married in 1930. I was born May 17, 1931 and my brother, Omar Edward "Eddie" was born April 2, 1933. Times were tough in the 1930s for my parents. For a short time, they managed the Dahlgren Hotel, and they actually served a banquet for the Governor of Illinois, Lewis L. Emmerson, who was visiting in the area sometime between 1929 and 1933. Here my facts are a little fuzzy because I'm relying on stories that were told to me by my parents and by friends who worked with my father and recalled some of these events to me much later.

The hotel experiment apparently did not last long and must have been a failure. Allen's Café survived, but soon the soda fountain was gone and efforts to stay afloat economically multiplied. In this period my parents raised chickens, milked cows, sold milk and raised pigs. During the 1930s my aunt Nell continued a full partner in the restaurant with my father, but <u>they did not get along</u>. As a little kid I witnessed some outstanding bouts of screaming and cussing between the two of them. She could cuss just as good as he, and that is saying a lot. Dad wanted to end his partnership with her for years, partly because he couldn't stand her and also because he wanted the income from the entire operation which he was splitting with her.

Dad initiated me into the operation of Allen's Café in 1941 when I was 10 years old. My main responsibility for a few years was primarily on Saturdays, our busiest day, washing dishes, racking the pool balls and collecting ten cents when one game ended and another began. The beginning of World War II in 1941 ushered in better economic times. For the first time since the 1920s our customers, mostly farmers, had more income and they were willing to spend some of it in Dahlgren. During the war, on Saturdays the town was full of horse-drawn vehicles of every imaginable type but mostly open wagons with lots of children in the wagon beds or buggies. Farmers were in town on Saturday to buy groceries, farm equipment and feed for the following week.

Every business in town did very well in the years of World War II, and so did Allen's Café. Saturday began for Dad and the rest of us sometime around 8 o'clock in the morning and lasted until 11 to 12 Saturday night. The store would be so full of people that it was hard to get through. By the end of the war in 1945 I had graduated to serving the ice cream parlor or when that did not occupy my time I would work behind the counter, rack pool balls and make sure there was plenty of cold Coke. He was told that he sold more Coca-Cola than any other business on the delivery route outside of Mount Vernon. Eddie by this time had inherited my responsibility as chief dishwasher and shared responsibility for racking pool balls.

A significant change for Dad and for the rest of us occurred in the summer of 1945 as the war ended. His sister Nell announced that she was getting married and agreed to sell her share of the store to Dad. Mom was very much opposed to this because she knew it meant that he would be in the store every day, and she was right. Dad ignored her objections, and from that summer on, until his retirement (probably in 1957 or 1958) he worked with occasional breaks every day, 8 a.m. to 10 p.m.

It is no exaggeration to say that Dad was one of the dominant personalities in Dahlgren during those years and one of the most successful businessmen. He was always known as "Petie Allen"; no one but his family ever called him Omar. He had a very quick sense of humor, and many times I have witnessed him entertaining customers sitting around the counter, laughing their heads off at something he had said or done, often at someone's expense. He had a nickname for every kid who came in the store, such as "Fasty," "Lightning," "Slop Bucket," or "Gun Barrel" and many others. Some of those nicknames stuck with the recipients the rest of their lives. He was lucky; he always won at cards and at pool. While he was not a particularly good pool shot, good things seemed always to happen for him and it was difficult to beat him.

There were two huge celebrations in Dahlgren the summer of 1945: the end of the war in Europe, May 8, 1945 and the shivaree for the marriage of Nell Allen to Walter Sneed on August 25, 1945. Both celebrations brought in huge numbers of people into the streets of Dahlgren directly in front of our Café. There were shotguns fired off at random through the evening, and a great deal of frolicking. It was hard to judge whether Aunt Nell's shivaree or the end of World War II in Europe received the greatest celebration, but it's safe I think to say that nothing like that has ever happened again in Dahlgren.

Soon after the war ended in 1945 the wartime prosperity for Dahlgren and much of small-town America came to an end. Dad's business quickly disappeared, and for that reason, but mainly because of his health, he closed Allen's Café permanently in the late 1950s.

Omar Ethan Allen, c. 1920

Omar Ethan Allen, c. 1922

The Allen Café, c. 1920s.   Nell Allen behind the counter.

Allen's Café, c.1930s

Petie Allen standing by the water jug. Nell Allen behind
the cash register. Standing on the left, probably Frank
Cross, who worked for them often in the 1930s.

Allen's Café, c. 1940s

"Petie Allen" standing behind the water jug. Customers at the counter are Leslie Miller, Elmer Irvin, and Wayne Starr (from Mt. Vernon).

Omar E. Allen with "Eddie" and Helen Allen with "Howard"

CHAPTER 8

HELEN WILSON ALLEN

Helen Marie Wilson, my mother, was born in Broughton, Illinois
in 1907. Her father, Robert Wilson, was a schoolteacher and a
farmer. He and his wife, Edith Brinkley Wilson, had a large
family. Three of their children, Sumner, Ruby and Edith, were a
product of his first marriage which ended in the death of his wife.
One, Vernon Singler, was Edith's son from her first marriage
which also ended in the death of her husband. Together Robert and
Edith had three additional children: Helen, Harold, and Arthur.

In the 1920s, Helen moved with her family from
McLeansboro, where her father worked as a teacher, to Dahlgren,
where Robert was hired as principal of the Dahlgren three-year
high school. I do not think that Mom ever went to Dahlgren high
school, but I do know for sure that her fourth year of high school
was completed in McLeansboro in 1924. During that year Mom
spent the entire week in McLeansboro living with her Aunt Susie
Black.

The next year she accepted a position as a teacher (she was
only 18 years old) in a rural, one-room school south of Dahlgren at
least 10 to 15 miles where she boarded during the school week
with the parents of students in the school. It was a very difficult
year for her and apparently very lonely, and she often talked about
it. Besides, roads were so bad that she was forced at times to ride a
horse from Dahlgren to where she boarded. A photograph of her
and her students in front of her one-room school is included; she
doesn't look much older than some of her students.

The following year, 1925 – 1926, she attended Southern
Illinois Normal College in Carbondale where she excelled in her
classes and played her violin in the college orchestra. She was by
this time a very talented violinist. She attended summer school in
1928, 1929 and 1930. During most of this time she continued to
live with her father in Dahlgren. In 1930 she met and married, O.

E. Allen. I was born the next year, 1931, and Eddie, in 1933. Mom spent the next six years at home raising Eddie and me.

In 1937 Mom accepted a job as the music teacher in the Dahlgren public grade school where she would teach until the late 1970s. I remember this pretty well, because I entered first grade the first year she taught, and I remember very well walking with her from our house to school on her first day of school and mine. I do not know the exact date she stopped teaching because long after she retired, she worked as a substitute teacher into the 1970s.

How Mom obtained this position is a mystery to me. It was always very significant to the financial health of the family even though her salary was very low. My suspicion is that Dad had influence with the school board. Music was rarely taught in the schools in southern Illinois, and Mom had minimal professional qualifications. There are two courses in music on her college transcript, and she had to teach herself to play the piano on the job. What she did have was a family background in music, she was a gifted violinist, and she was very anxious to do well. And so, she did. Not only did she teach classes in music for several years after World War II, but she organized a school orchestra and welcomed high school students to play along with students in the grade school. The year that I was in the eighth grade she organized a small music group of grade schoolers of about six or seven players which so impressed my grandfather, who in the meantime had been elected Hamilton County Superintendent of Schools, to take our little orchestra to provide entertainment at grade school graduation ceremonies in the county.

In the years that followed almost no public Dahlgren event, high school or grade school ceremony or performance occurred without Mom's name on the program. She became an excellent self–taught pianist, and a very popular teacher. At some point in the 1950s (after I left home) she was assigned to teach fifth grade and the music program was abolished. This does not mean that she had abandoned her commitment to music, and many demands were made on her for her musical talents into the 1970s even after she retired. She played piano and organ most Sundays at the Methodist

Church; organized Christmas Cantatas, and provided music for dozens of funeral services.

A memorable demonstration of her impact on the Dahlgren community occurred sometime probably in the 1990s when a reunion of all alumni of the Dahlgren public schools was held in Mt. Vernon with an enormous crowd, estimated to be 500 alumni. When Mom was introduced to the crowd, the entire audience, all 500 alumni, jumped to their feet and applauded!

Almost everyone who lived in Dahlgren from the 1930s to the 1990s "went to school with Miss Allen" and most remember taking her classes or performing in some of her programs. This kind of legacy makes teaching a very satisfactory career.

Helen Marie Wilson's first school class, 1925

Helen Marie Wilson, c. 1920s.

Dahlgren Public School Orchestra, 1943

Helen Marie Allen, c. 1975

CHAPTER 9

SOME GENERALIZATIONS AND SPECULATION

In this closing section I would like to raise some questions and
speculations about the results I have included in this document.
What was Hamilton County like when my ancestors arrived here
and how did they end up in Hamilton County? According to the
United States Census, the county in 1830 had a population of 2,616
when the Josiah Allen family arrived in the late 1830s. Hamilton
County is located near the northern center of the southern Illinois
counties, and it is a considerable distance away from any
significant river or waterway. In the years before the development
of the railway system, population centers and development of
towns was located on the rivers--the Mississippi, the Ohio, the
Wabash and the Big Muddy. So, few people were attracted to
Hamilton County, and a lot of that area was still unclaimed federal
land in the 1830s and 1840s. According to my grandfather's
memoirs, land was still heavily forested when he grew up near
Texas City in Saline County in the 1880s, years after the Civil
War. So, for Josiah Allen and William B. Allen, and the Ingram
family, Hamilton County would have been an area where farmland
was still unclaimed from the federal government and available for
purchase. And, in fact, in April 1830 Josiah Allen purchased from
the federal government 80 acres of land at $1.25 per acre in
Section 22 (W2SE, Township 11N, Range 12W), located
approximately three miles west of McLeansboro and very near the
location of Ten Mile Church.[29] I am not familiar with the process
of purchasing land from the federal government in the 1830s, but I
believe that this required a trip to the federal land office in

---

[29] Josiah Allen purchased an additional 40 acres on July 8, 1838
(Southwest quarter of the Northeast quarter of Section Thirteen in
Township 5S, Range 5E), and his son, William B. Allen, also
bought land in 1848 and 1851 as did his son Calvin Young Allen
in 1853. Sewel Ingram also purchased land in 1841, 1851,1850.

Shawneetown, a long trip in those days. And how could Josiah have had at his command $100 in cash in an economy which was predominantly subsistence, where most transactions were bartered and hard cash scarce? These conditions would have been especially severe for a nomadic family that had been on the move from North Carolina almost continuously for a decade.

A second fact which fascinates me is that almost all of my ancestors, except for most of the Wilson family, were Southerners and almost all of them from the Appalachian counties of North Carolina. By my count eight male ancestors were born in Appalachian North Carolina, and Thomas Marsh, born in Warren County, Tennessee, and David Crunk, born in Posey County, Indiana, were sons of fathers born in Appalachian North Carolina.

Not much is known about these Southerners who settled in Hamilton County, but we do have the federal censuses which beginning in 1850, are very rich in information, and we have the county level election returns for these counties. Hamilton County before the Civil War voted in very similar ways to most voters in the southern counties of Illinois, Indiana and Ohio. Until after the end of World War II in 1945 Hamilton County was overwhelmingly Democratic. It cast 96.1% of its vote for Democrat Andrew Jackson in 1828, and the Democratic presidential vote margin did not fall below 75% until 1868 when the vote for the Republican candidate did enjoy a modest 38.7% of the vote.

Hamilton County voted overwhelmingly against Abraham Lincoln in 1860 when he only received 5.8% of the popular vote. The historical record, both the election returns and a great deal of additional historical documents, demonstrate conclusively that the majority of the population in the county was either opposed to or at least unwilling to support the Union cause during the Civil War. The Republican governor of Illinois during the Civil War, Richard Yates, made strenuous efforts to support Illinois troops under federal control throughout the war. In this effort he was seriously obstructed and denounced by the leaders of the Democratic Party in the Illinois legislature and elsewhere. This anti-Union sentiment was widespread among Democrats in most of the southern counties of Illinois, Indiana and Ohio. They call themselves "peace Democrats," but Unionists often referred to them as "Copperheads."[30]

Hamilton County was a "Copperhead" county. Not only did Hamilton County voters support Democratic candidates for election to the state legislature in 1862 at 79.4%, but in the absolutely critical presidential election of 1864 Hamilton County gave 75% of its vote for the Democratic candidate, former General George B. McClellan, a peace Democrat who favored an end to the Civil War and probably secession of the Confederacy. Across southern Illinois during the war there was a considerable degree of opposition to the war and even some violence, but I am not familiar with any hard evidence of violence in Hamilton County. I do recall a story I was told by an elderly gentleman I met in the County Courthouse in the 1950s. He remembered that there had been a band of deserters camped in what was then a swampy area in eastern Hamilton County that was raided by a union Calvary unit sometime during the war.

While the great majority of the population in Hamilton County was opposed to the Civil War, there was a minority that was not. On April 12, 1861 Confederate forces in South Carolina opened fire on Fort Sumter, and three days later President Lincoln declared the existence of an insurrection and called for 75,000 troops. The 6th, Illinois Cavalry Regiment was officially organized in Camp Butler Illinois in November 1861 and moved to Shawneetown, Illinois that same month. However, Company D of that regiment was already organized in McLeansboro on the 11th day of October, 1861 when both William B. Allen and his brother James Allen enlisted in Company D. Thomas Marsh also enlisted in Company D on the same day. Three representatives of the

---

[30] Robert P. Howard, <u>Illinois: A History of the Prairie State</u> (Grand Rapids Michigan: William B. Eerdmans Publishing Company), 307-316. Wayne Edson Stevens, "A Study of Southern Illinois Politics During the Civil War" (master's thesis, University of Illinois, 1914). 63-86.

Ingram family and one member of the Brinkley family are also on the manifest of Company D. Chances are they also enlisted on August 11, 1861.

A rough count of the manifest of Company D suggests that approximately ninety-two of the 145 members of the Company provided a McLeansboro mailing address which indicates that most of the members of the Company were neighbors and/or lived pretty close together. The enlistment of recruits in the western part of the county in Union Army units is also suggested by a rough count of the members and mailing addresses of a second unit recruited in the same area. Company A of the 40th Illinois Infantry was recruited overwhelmingly from Knights Prairie Township, Lovilla and Macedonia. Eighty-nine of the 110 recruits of that company were from that area. In other words, in the two companies examined the recruits were concentrated primarily in a region of the county just west of McLeansboro, and only a few individuals from other parts of the county. There was also a scattering of others from Benton, Mount Vernon and other local towns. But in Company D of the 6th Illinois Calvary and Company A of the 40th Illinois Infantry the concentration of recruits was clearly in McLeansboro, Knights Prairie Township and Lovilla. I found very few names and addresses in the very north west section of the county or in the township's from north east to south east of McLeansboro.[31]

This discovery raises some interesting observations about the behavior of the population in Hamilton County and the political record in the years that would follow, and it provides for some very interesting speculation. One question: why were the Union recruits in Company D and Company A found primarily in one section of the county? My guess is that somehow there was a system of communication among these poor farmers that led them

---

[31] Carol Lee Yarbrough, "The Yesterdays of Hamilton County, Illinois, carolyar.com/Illinois/Hamilton County.htm.

to settle in parts of the west together and that they shared common values. Probably there was some kind of chain migration going on here about which I have no knowledge, although the literature on the westward movement suggests that there was communication between early settlers and those who came later. In some areas there were also efforts made by large land speculators and local boosters to recruit settlers. Perhaps those who came into the county early wrote to family back in the eastern states to encourage them to come to Hamilton County.[32] That may explain this settlement pattern, but I have no existing record of any such letters or communications.

During the work on the voting history of Hamilton County in the 1930s and 1940s for my Master's degree I found precinct level election returns for the elections from 1932 to 1945 in the Hamilton County records. By plotting these returns on maps of Hamilton County I was able to demonstrate that the county was very Democratic and strongly supported Franklin D. Roosevelt in all four of his elections: 1932, 1936, 1940 and 1944. In the same four elections there was a solid and consistent Republican vote in the county. It was concentrated solidly in the precincts which included McLeansboro, Knights Prairie Township and Dahlgren Township. Lovilla by the 1930s had long since been abandoned when what would become known as the Louisville and Nashville Railroad was built through Hamilton County in the 1870s and created a railroad stop at a new village, Dahlgren.

The residents of this Unionist concentration in the western sections of the county were largely from the South, as were the residence of the rest of the county, but there was certainly a difference. My guess is that this part of the county was settled by farm families from Appalachian counties where there was a deep hostility or resentment to the plantation aristocracy that dominated the states they had left. The Appalachian counties in West

---

[32] Douglas K. Meyer, <u>Making the Heartland Quilt.</u> 12-13.

Virginia, East Tennessee, North Carolina and North Eastern Georgia provided substantial numbers of Union troops during the Civil War just as did their former neighbors who settled in Hamilton County, Illinois. As late as the 1940s the Republican party was quite strong and carried many counties in Appalachia. As V. O. Key observed in his classic study of southern politics, "Tennessee's Democratic/Republican cleavage stands as a monument to the animosities of Civil War and Reconstruction. Even before the War a sense of separatism set off East Tennesseans from their fellow citizens to the west."[33] It was very much the same in the mountain counties of North Carolina and in some of the western townships in Hamilton County, Illinois.

What I am suggesting is that the divisions and hostility of the Civil War era had a major impact on the voting behavior and probably many other parts of the culture of Hamilton County, Illinois at least until after World War II. It's not so surprising when you think about it; it has not been that long ago. My grandfather Robert Wilson knew a Captain in the Indiana Volunteers, his father. My dad remembered, barely, his grandfather, Thomas Marsh, who served as a sergeant in the Illinois cavalry. Robert Wilson's mother received a Civil War pension until she died in the 1920s. Thomas Marsh's widow received a federal pension until she died in 1922. The memories of the war, the deaths of those who did not come back, and the financial relief in the form of federal pensions for Union veterans and their families, all this cemented an enduring family loyalty to the Republican Party.

This is very interesting to me since I know that every ancestor I have uncovered that lived during the Civil War became a Unionist and a Republican. And in growing up in the 1930s around both my Wilson family and my Allen family there was no doubt that we were devout Republicans. It was almost like a religion rather than a political identification. There was a strong

---

[33] V. O. Key, <u>Southern Politics in State and Nation</u> (New York: Alfred A. Knopf, 1950), 75.

conviction that there was a moral difference between Republicans and Democrats – – the Republicans were righteous, Democrats were different. The Civil War was often remembered especially by my mother and Abraham Lincoln was regarded with almost religious devotion. I suspect that this conception of the Republican Party was widespread across most rural communities in small towns in the Northeast and the Midwest where Union troops were recruited. I think it is still the case that where ever you find counties in the states that supported the Union in the 1860s and that have not experienced substantial industrialization or urbanization since the 1860s, in other words still pretty rural, relatively speaking, the majorities still vote Republican.

So, in Hamilton County, during and long after the Civil War, a majority of the residents in Knights Prairie, McLeansboro and Dahlgren Township Republicans were a minority, perhaps even a persecuted minority. During the years of Civil War and for decades later, as long as the generation of this war lived, there must have been expressions of hostility and conflict, perhaps even violence, between the Unionists (Republicans) and their Democratic (Copperhead) neighbors It was after all a very bloody, ugly, brutal war in which there were approximately 850,000 casualties, and many who survived the war died young from exposure, disease and disabilities (like the case of William B. Allen), or who suffered from emotional or psychological effects of the war which, in those years, was not a recognized medical disability.

I must also point out that this speculation about connections between the Civil War and loyalty to the Republican Party among Appalachian farmers who settled in in Hamilton County do not apply to the Wilson family. The Wilson's were not from the South, and after 1800 this family was concentrated in the farms surrounding New Harmony, Indiana. Recall the connection between Lewis Wilson and the leader of the Rapp community in Pennsylvania, and later in the New Harmony settlement. Given what we know about the dedication to social reform and the promotion of science and learning under the influence of Robert Dale Owen and his successors in New Harmony, there must have been powerful anti-slavery and even abolitionist sentiment in the area. Some of this may have influenced the Wilson family and Isaac Wilson, his brother, Luther, and their cousin, Alexander Stallings, to promptly enlist in the Union army in 1861. Or, possibly their anti-slavery values were already a part of their world view, acquired by earlier generations of Wilsons who had lived in Pennsylvania or perhaps even earlier.

I cannot lay my hands at this moment on election returns in Posey County during the Civil War, but Wood Gray in <u>The Hidden Civil War</u> provides a series of maps showing the county distribution of Midwestern Civil War state elections, and while in nearly all southern Indiana counties a majority voted for the Democratic party in all of these elections, at least one, perhaps two counties in the area of Posey County, voted Republican.[34] Given the social and cultural history of New Harmony, it makes sense that this area would be antislavery, Republican and Unionist. My guess is that the New Harmony influence was a major factor in the Wilson family's commitment to the Union cause.

But this much I know for sure, the Wilson clan had a stronger commitment to learning and love for music than most of the settlers in Hamilton County, including the Allen family, who took little to no special interest in learning and music and was primarily committed to hard work and making a living. I remember my grandfather Wilson often telling me about spelling bees and cipher bees that were part of the entertainment going on near his father's farm near Texas City. Also, in his Memoirs my grandfather mentioned the musical talents of his mother's father, his mother's beautiful singing voice, and he remembered that his father played the fiddle in community dances, a fiddle which still is in the family. Robert also played the fiddle, and he recorded a large collection of folksongs he learned from his mother, songs I have

---

[34] Wood Gray, <u>The Hidden Civil War: The Story of the Copperheads</u> (New York: The Viking Press,1964). 32, 61, 109, 152, and 205.

often heard him sing, recordings which are now deposited in the National Archives. Although he only went to public school two years in his life, my grandfather had a great love of literature, American and British, and even in his last years he could recite long passages from Sir Walter Scott's "The Lady of the Lake" for me. Grandpa Wilson was also a talented artist as his drawing of his family log cabin where he grew up illustrates. He drew up the plans for at least two barns that I am aware of, and he was also very talented in mathematics. I was not, and in my freshman year at Southern Illinois University I was having difficulties with word problems in Algebra One. In those days we students at SIUC went home on weekends, and for several weeks I spent my Saturday mornings with Grandpa Wilson as he showed me how to compute word problems in algebra. I was extremely impressed with my grandfather at the time, and with the passage of time and experience I am even more overwhelmed today with his intellect and achievements. As one of his sons said to me once, "if Dad had been born anywhere but where he was born in rural, isolated Southern Illinois, there is no way to know how much he could have achieved." He left behind children, grandchildren, and great-grandchildren who are musicians, teachers, and story tellers and that legacy is still continuing—an outstanding legacy indeed.

O. E. (Eddie) Allen and Howard Wilson Allen, c.1950s

Sources

Brown, Alexander. Grierson's Raid. A Cavalry Adventure of the Civil War. Urbana: University of Illinois Press, 1962.

Gray, Wood. The Hidden Civil War: The Story of the Copperheads. New York: The Viking Press, 1964.

History of Butler County, Pennsylvania R. G. Brown & Company, Chicago, 1895.

"History of the Descendants of Lewis Wilson." Compiled by Judge Herdis P. Clements for the Wilson Reunion-August 1, 1937 at New Harmony, Indiana.

Howard, Robert P. Illinois: A History of the Prairie State. Grand Rapids Michigan: William B. Eerdmans Publishing Company.

Key, V. O. Southern Politics in State and Nation. New York: Alfred A. Knopf, 1950.

March, Delores Eckroat. "In Retrospect Wilson." 1998, updated 2006.

McCullough, David, The Heroic Story of the Settlers Who Brought the American Ideal West. New York: Simon and Schuster, 2019.

"The Memoirs of Robert Wilson," copy in my possession.

Meyer, Douglas K. Making the Heartland Quilt. A Geographical History of Settlement and Migration in Early-Nineteenth-Century Illinois. Carbondale and Edwardsville: Southern Illinois University Press, 2000.

Morris, Richard B. and Morris, Jeffrey B. (eds.), Encyclopedia of American History (New York, 7th Edition, 1996).

"New Harmony," <u>Encyclopedia Britannica</u> (Revised and updated by Amy Tikkanen, 2020), https:www.britannica.com/place /New Harmony.

Roberts, Merritt E. <u>Roberts-Allen Families and Related Families Davis, Highfill, Rogers</u>. Oliver Press Publications, 1985.

60th Regimental Infantry (3 Years Service). <u>Report of the Adjutant General of the State of Indiana,1865</u>.

Stevens, Wayne Edson. "A Study of Southern Illinois Politics During the Civil War." Master's thesis, University of Illinois, 1914, pp. 63-86.

Watson, Alan D. 1974. The Ferry in Colonial North Carolina: A Vital Link in Transportation. <u>The North Carolina Historical Review</u> 51: 247-260.

Appendix 1

THE MEMOIRS OF ROBERT WILSON

Foreword by Howard Allen, Robert Wilson's grandson

Robert Wilson (1876-1957) was born in Texas City, Saline County, Illinois and spent most of his adult life in Hamilton County. His father was Isaac Wilson (1834-1906), a farmer who served as a 1st Lt. in the 60th Indiana Infantry during the Civil War, and his mother was Martha Crunk Wilson (1849-1925). Both are buried in Mt. Oval Church Cemetery in White County. As he describes it in the following document, the region where he was born was still a frontier well after the end of the Civil War. Robert Wilson attended public school only very briefly and college only one summer session after he was 40, but he was an exceptionally literate, self-educated adult. He was highly skilled in mathematics and algebra and could quote lengthy excerpts from the Bible and the works of authors such as Sir Walter Scott, Henry Wadsworth Longfellow and John Greenleaf Whittier. He was also an authority on folk songs, most of which he learned from his mother, Martha Crunk Wilson. Recordings of many of these songs were recorded and are preserved in the National Archives of the United States. He taught at various schools in Hamilton County, served as Superintendent of the McLeansboro City Schools, principal of the Broughton and Dahlgren High Schools, and as County Superintendent of Schools in Hamilton County from 1938 to 1946. (See "Students Hold 'Bob Wilson Day' at Dahlgren" in "The Yesterdays of Hamilton County.")

BIRTHPLACE

If you go about a mile and a half west on a gravel road out of the little town of Texas City in Southern Illinois, you will notice a narrow lane running south. Go down that lane about a quarter of a mile and you will be even with the spot where I was born. As you face south the little log house which was my first earthly home stood about two hundred yards to your left in what is now an open field.

It has been more than sixty years since we left that spot for good, but the picture in my memory is about as clear and well defined as any I am able to produce. Let me imagine that I am seven years old and have just stopped at the place mentioned. There, at my left, are the bars. Beyond the bars is the Front Lot surrounded on three sides by a rail fence, on the fourth side is a high paling fence, and back of that fence stands the house. And what a house: Any seven-year-old boy nowadays would consider it almost a calamity to have to live in such a house. It was a log house with a big shed-like porch running its full length on the west, with a side-room, or lean-to kitchen on the east. A log smoke house stood just east of the kitchen, and a stick-and-clay chimney stood at the north end. The main room of the house was of hewed logs. These logs had been cut and hewed from big trees and were broad, carefully matched, and fitted together at the ends, making rather neat, straight up and down corners, and leaving small cracks between. These cracks were chinked and daubed with clay. The chimney at the north end of the house was built entirely without brick or stone, and consisted of a big wide base—which was just a wooden pen of notched timbers, with an inside lining of clay a foot or two thick, making the fireplace. The top or throat of the chimney was much smaller than the base and was built on sticks rived, or riven, out of parts of the body of trees, making a tall pen which was lined thickly with clay. The jambs and hearth of the big fireplace inside were built of clay and were easily damaged by a blow from the big fire poker or by letting a stick of firewood fall against them. However, while they were easily damaged, they were easily repaired. All you had to do was get a shovel full of clay, wet it to the consistency of stiff mud and daub up the break.

The roof was of boards rived with a fro. The ceiling, or loft, was of the same kind. The floors were of coarse unplanned plank and never had a carpet or rug on them. South of the yard and the Front Lot was the horse-lot and log stable. This stable was a sorry sort of shelter for horses or cows in winter. The cracks between the logs were not chinked and daubed and the poor animals inside must have suffered severely in winter weather. The chicken house stood just north of the stable and consisted of a rail pen built on posts set in the ground, standing about four feet high. One can imagine the comfort afforded chickens in such a shelter on a cold night.

Such is a very brief picture of my birthplace. When I look at this scene in memory many little details come into view. If it is summer, there are the tall ironweeds in the front lot—the thick woods with their big trees and tangled underbrush just across the narrow lane on the right. The small fields of my father's farm which he had cleared from the forest—the tall dark wall of timber surrounding this little farm, the deadening of big trees where the underbrush had been cleared away so that corn could be raised among the dead trees and stumps. There is the straw shed off to the left there near the old crooked elm tree, and just south of the house the thicket (Goldsmith[35] would call it a copse) of plum sprouts, and near the thicket the old well.

Let me stop here a moment to tell you something that almost happened to me in connection with this plum sprout thicket. It seems that my father was taking special care of these plum sprouts, expecting, no doubt, to transplant the best ones so as to have some fresh fruit. Once, I remember, some kinfolks of ours visited us from back in Indiana where our parents came from. As I recall, two stalwart young men, my father's cousins— I think it was Med and Lute Stallings[36]. They evidently were

---

[35] Oliver Goldsmith (1730-1774), Anglo-Irish author and playwright.

heroic sort of fellows, for one of them related very enthusiastically the story of a fight he had witnessed. It must have been between one of his friends and another man—but at any rate at a certain place in the story he demonstrated right before us all and the big fireplace how one of the fellows had lunged at the other one with a big knife, and uttering a lot of big swear words proceeded to do him bad. I don't remember just how the fight ended but I do recall that the whole thing impressed me immensely. Next day it was still seething in my mind. I armed myself with mother's big butcher knife and went out to find an enemy I could cut down. The first enemy I saw happened to be those fine plum sprouts. I distinctly recall how they incited me to fight. I would get set and then suddenly rush at one of those sprouts, uttering big oaths, and would deliberately hack it to pieces. My father discovered the havoc I had wrought next day— or perhaps that same day—and as I remember now—my memory suffered a severe lapse—I couldn't remember seeing anybody about those plum sprouts all day.

Along the south of the smokehouse was a shed, and under the eaves of the shed there usually stood a big trough my father had hewed or dug out of the body of a tree. It was an enormously big trough, or so it seems to me now, and my mother used to keep her homemade soap in it—so we always called it the soap trough. When it was empty of soap they set it under the eaves of the smokehouse shed to catch rain water.

Just south of the house was the well, and near by just inside the horse lot near the fence was the watering trough. This was a dugout trough like the soap-trough. I remember one day when I was very small my father and his brother, my Uncle Luther[37], came up to the watering trough with their teams of tired

---

[36] Isaac Wilson's mother was Sabrina Stallings (1803-?); the cousins mentioned here were probably her Grandsons from the New Harmony, Indiana area.

horses. I remember that I got to wondering what caused a well, and I asked my father how he got the well.   He told me they dug it. I then asked him how they dug a well—my uncle said "With the hatchet."

For a long time, I wondered how anybody could dig a well with a hatchet. This and many other similar questionings which bothered my childish mind come up often to remind me, in a small way, of how a little child learns—and how what we consider commonplace and simple is sometimes a great mystery to the child. I am sure that some of the great blunders I have made in trying to teach children are due to my failure or in-ability to realize that I am dealing with a person whose every experience is a new one, and presents problems as foreign to their understanding as Hebrew and Sanskrit would be to me.

East of the horse-lot was a small field in which were a few apple trees. These were very few; I remember only two, the Horse-apple, and the Strawberry. The strawberries were early apples and they are the only ones, as I recall, that ever got any ways near ripe, we boys would eat them all up long before they could ripen. Our parents tried to prevent this and laid down certain rules which they hoped would have the desired results. We were permitted to eat the apples what fell from the trees. Evidently, they could not trust us always to be fair so the rules soon required that all apples be brought to them for inspection before we could eat them. If the stem end of the apple was brown that was accepted as proof that we had found the apple on the ground and had not pulled it off the tree. If the stem end was fresh and green it proved that we had pulled the apple. My brother[38] was resourceful lad and he wasn't long in concocting a

---

[37] Luther Wilson (1840-1899), Isaac's brother, also served in the 60th Indiana Infantry during the Civil War. He is buried at Mt. Oval Church Cemetery in White County.

[38] Probably Allie Jesse Wilson (1874-?), Robert's older brother.

plan to overcome this handicap. He would slip out, pull off a few apples and hide them behind the smokehouse for a few hours until the stem end turned brown, and then take them in for inspection. My recollection is that our mother was not long in finding this out.

This incident will help to show some of the hardships of pioneer life. Our home was in a really new country. Few people for miles around had any fruit trees, and ripe apples, peaches, plums etc., were rare luxuries. In the big woods could be found wild plums, grapes, haws, crab apples, and berries, but even these things were hard to get at our place, and the delicious canned fruit we enjoy now was unknown.

Life was decidedly of the pioneer type. The descriptions of pioneer life which our children read in school and library books give a true picture of life as I experienced it as a boy. To be sure, most of the pioneer homes described in books were far superior to my boyhood home. Many of the early pioneer homes had wide fireplaces built of stone or brick with many added conveniences such as a crane, a built-in oven, or a Dutch oven. They had fine hand-carved mantel boards, sideboards, staircases, attics, etc. Our home was crude and rough. My father built it entirely with his own hands and with very few tools. He was not a trained workman and, having been used to primitive comforts all his life, seemed never to long for more than the bare necessities.

I wouldn't for anything, intentionally leave the impression that I look back upon my boyhood in that crude and hard environment with vain regrets, or with any feeling that I was deprived of something because of it, to which I was by nature entitled. It never occurred to me then that I was in any sense unfortunate because of my station in life. I am not sure that I would have been happier if I had been born in a wealthy home in a modern community surrounded by every advantage and comfort life could afford. I am not sure that I would have taken any better advantage of my opportunities if my environment had been different. Life, Fate, or Destiny, or whatever we call it, it seems to me, has a mysterious way of putting it into a person, somehow, someway either to overcome his environment or to be overcome by it. Somewhere, at some critical point, in every one's life something happens to him which either makes or breaks him as far as mastering his own circumstance is concerned. If the education of children we are told that there are three principal outcomes to strive for, (1) knowledge, (2) skills, and (3) attitudes, and of these, attitudes are probably of greatest importance and no doubt the most difficult to attain if true excellence in terms of life's real values is the aim. The highest aim in this life is true happiness. Our happiness is conditioned more by our attitudes than by any other thing. If we look upon our condition in life with too great a degree of melancholy we cannot be happy no matter how favorable that condition. If we look upon our condition with a cheerful, optimistic, contented, attitude, we can be extremely happy no matter how unfavorable that condition.

When I was a boy, I heard very little complaining around the fireside at home about anything. The neighbors were always fine folks—the weather was never so bad that it might not have been worse—the strangers who stopped for the night—and my father very seldom turned one away—were never censured. I never knew but what the home I was bred and born in was the finest best home in the world—and to me it was just that. I am trying to analyze those events and forces in my early childhood that had the greatest influence in shaping my life. Nothing in my childhood experience—as I can recall—ever induced in me the attitude of self-pity. I am glad I had parents who left their children in most cases to their own resources. If I fell down and hurt myself, I was told to get up and go ahead—not be a crybaby. If I didn't get just what I wanted when playing with other children I was not led by an over-indulgent parent to feel that I had been mistreated. I unconsciously learned to abide by my mother's oft-expressed philosophy that what can't be cured must be endured. The tender care and kindly sympathy of loving parents were not denied me when I needed them but they were bestowed in such a way as to lead me gradually to feel and realize that I received them not because and when my selfish fancy demanded them but when I needed and deserved them. I am happy to believe that such wholesome influences induced in me, on the whole, proper attitudes. I never assumed the attitude that the world or anybody owed me a living. I have always felt that I was the debtor, that I had already, at any point in life, received more than my share of the good things, and my job was to do something worthwhile to (as my mother would say) pay for my salt.

It has been said that a child's education should begin with his grandfather. That is to say that a child's education is well begun if he had good parents, and I feel that I had good parents. Neither one of my parents was a descendant of noted people. So far as I know none of their ancestors came over in the Mayflower or were related to Pocahontas. My father's name was Isaac, and naturally went by the name of Ike. He was born in Posey County in Southern Indiana. I have heard him say that he attended a school a total of nine days, three days each to three different teachers. He often said he could remember only one incident in connection with his school days that was when a wasp flew down from its nest on a rafter of the old log schoolhouse and stung a girl pupil on the finger. In spite of this lack of schooling my father was a pretty fair scholar. I remember that the neighbors for miles round our home used to bring their important letters and business papers to our house for father to read and write answers for them. He was pretty good in arithmetic and could gauge a wagon bed or grain bin, or compute land area. He was not especially enthusiastic about his children getting more than the rudiments of an education, yet he showed in a very quiet way, the usual parent's pride in us when we did well in school. He objected to spending money for the extra books when my teacher wanted me to begin the study of grammar and physiology. He rather reluctantly bought me an advanced arithmetic, but when I got into a list of difficult problems and the whole school got stuck on one, he got so interested that he got up one winter night in the middle of the night, hunted up my slate and pencil and worked an hour or so on that problem. He thought he had worked out the solution. He hadn't. We finally worked it though. I forget whether he or I got it first.

While, as I said in a previous paragraph, my father was

not a trained workman, there were some things he could do well. I have heard his neighbors say he was one of the best wheat cradlers in the neighborhood, and he could play the old-time tunes on the fiddle better than any other person I ever heard. His father's name was David. [39] He was born in Posey County, Indiana, in 1800 and died in October 1876, about a month before I was born. Grandfather David Wilson was a pretty well-educated man considering the times and opportunities offered a poor man's son then. He taught school and was a country lawyer, serving several years as justice of the peace. I remember when I was a small boy I had his justice-of-the peace court docket to play with, and not realize what a rare relic I would have considered it could I have it now, I tore it up and destroyed it. I remember yet the quaint writing and its faded and yellowed pages. Without doubt the writing in it was done with a homemade quill pen and with homemade ink.

My father's grandfather's name was Lewis. He emigrated from Ireland probably about 1760, and settled in Pennsylvania. We have never been able to learning anything about his family in Ireland but it is pretty certain that he came to America when he was about 12 years old as a stow-away.[40] Father's mother came to Posey County, Indiana from North Carolina with her parents probably about the year 1815. She was then 12 years old. Her

---

[39] David Wilson (1800-1876) was born in Butler County, Pennsylvania and moved to the New Harmony, Indiana area with his father, Lewis Wilson (1760?-1850) sometime between 1810 and 1820.

[40] Lewis Wilson appears in the U.S. Census of 1800 in Butler County, Pennsylvania. At that time, he was married with seven children. He was between the ages 26 and 45, which suggests that Robert was approximately correct in placing Lewis' birth date at 1760. Lewis was still alive in Posey County in 1845 when he purchased 40 acres from the federal government.

maiden name was Stallings. Stallings were Scotch Irish people who settled in the mountainous western parts of Virginia and the Carolinas, later crossing the mountain into Kentucky and Tennessee then into Southern Indiana, and Illinois along with Daniel Boone, George Rogers Clark, and other hardy pioneers. The Stallings brought a number of slaves with them from North Carolina. These, of course, became free when their owners brought them north of the Ohio River. I've often heard my father speak of these old Negroes, who, lived along with their old owners. One old Negro, especially, whose name was Hawk, taught my father to play many of the old-time fiddle tunes he knew. Some of these tunes evidently had originated among the French settlers along the lower Mississippi. Most of them, however, where from the old Irish, Scotch, or, English.

I never knew much about my mother's people or their ancestry. Her maiden name was Crunk. Her father was a singing teacher of the old school. He taught note reading in the old Southern Harmony system of shaped notes and conducted singing classes. I am sure he did not depend on this as a means of livelihood, but as a means of social enjoyment and advancement. My mother's family were honorable respected citizens of more than average intelligence and culture in the neighborhoods where they lived. None of them acquired much wealth but none of them was extremely poor. They owned farms or comfortable homes and lived quite well. I suppose I am justified in saying I believe my mother was a remarkable person in many respects. I believe she had a really fine singing voice, and while I have no means of knowing for sure, it is my opinion that few women anywhere or any time could reach higher notes than she could. Her voice was sweet and very musical yet very strong and powerful. Many times, I remember near sundown, she would be caring for the milk cows and calves at the bars in the Front Lot and invariably singing some of the many songs she knew by heart. She could sing from memory every line of scores of old-time songs—folk songs, religious songs, almost any kind. The poet says: "Of all the beautiful pictures//That Hang on memory's walls …." [words missing] with me, the one of my mother going about her evening chores on a clear still evening about sundown and singing in her fine clear strong voice which, I am sure, could be heard a mile or more "seemeth the best of all."

My mother was strong and active. She was a very good horseback rider and many a ride have I taken on the old sorrel mare behind her, holding on to her with both hands while she went at a brisk trot or gallop. I have heard her tell of the many races she had with the neighboring boys and girls when she was young and everybody went to church or neighborhood parties on horseback. She always rode with the old-time sidesaddle.

As I have said before, the whole region round about where I lived as a child was covered with dense forest. The soil was rich black bottom and the trees were of many kinds and sizes; some of them of great size and height. One kind which I remember especially they called the Turkey Oak. It was a tall straight bodied tree and sometimes grew very large. It was prized very highly by the old timers because of its quality of being easily split into rails or boards. Another tree of much value was the sweet gum. Aside from its value as a lumber tree and for firewood, it was prized by us children as a source of chewing gum. The sap from the sweet gum would flow from a wound made by an ax and collect in masses. We children would gather this wax and chew it the same as children (and other folks) nowadays chew spearmint or Wrigley's. Most of the space between the big trees was occupied with small shrubs and dense undergrowth. In some places hazel bushes grew thickly and we could gather great quantities of these delicacies in the fall. Big scaly-bark hickories were plentiful and the big nuts could be gathered by the wagon loads along the creeks. Dogwoods were plentiful and the woodsmen used the wood of these small trees to make wedges or gluts, as [words missing] …. while green and the gluts were shaped with a sharp ax and laid away to season. After seasoning these gluts of dogwood were almost as hard as iron and would stand a log of mauling before splitting.

The big woods abounded in wild game, as coons, foxes, mink, weasels, squirrels, etc. A few wild turkeys still lived deep in the woods along the creek, and occasionally a flock of them could be seen in the cornfields late in the fall or early winter where they had come out in search of food. One morning in the dead of winter after a heavy snowfall, a big turkey gobbler came out of the woods near our house, and ran across our field to the woods on the other side. He had to cross three high fences which he did with apparent ease—hopping on top of each one and down on the other side with little effort. My older brother and I went out to look at his tracks in the snow. We tried to step in them and found we could not jump from one of his tracks to the other. One evening near sundown a big wild turkey was discovered in our garden. The fence round the garden was of tall palings and the turkey was unable to get out. My father took our dog, Cricket, into the garden and together they caught the turkey, which had been shot by a hunter and had a wing injured so it couldn't fly. My mother was preparing to heat water for dressing the turkey when two hunters came up on hunt of their pretty, which, it turned out, they had shot and broke its wing. The turkey was in the top of a tall tree not far away and had sailed down from the tree, landing in our garden where father caught it. On several occasions we had wild turkey meat for dinner.

The big woods always induced in me a sense of awe and mystery. I remember going with my brother to the edge of the woods not far from our house. I must have been not more than four, and, while the distance to the woods was not more than a few rods it seemed a long way to me. We had our dog with us and, as I remember, the day was dark, rather cold and windy. Our dog treed a rabbit in a brush pile, and my brother climbed upon the brush to run the rabbit out. Pretty soon out came old rabbit with the dog yelping after him and my brother following and yelling. I was frightened. I was left alone by the big woods with the wind roaring in the tall tree tops. The loneliness was oppressive. The big world, the big woods, the unknown mysteries all but overcame me. It made a lasting impression which I have never completely lost. Was it Byron who said, "There is a pleasure in the pathless woods; There is rapture on the lonely shore; There is society where none intrudes, By the deep sea, and music in its roar."[41] I always like to listen to the sounds of the woods. I have listened to the squirrels barking, the laughing and hooting of the owls. I have heard the peculiar sounds made by minks as they would prowl round our house on a winter night. I knew the tracks of the coons, the possums, the squirrels, the foxes.

My earliest experience with books and reading was with little ABC picture books. These were usually of linen and had ABC rhymes and appropriate pictures. The pictures were wonderful things to me. I can still feel some of the thrill I got from enjoying them, especially fascinating to me were the bright colors. Sometimes in my experience as a teacher I would try to draw on my childhood experience to help me better to understand the little children under my care, and better provide for their development and training—and my recollection of how the bright colored pictures in those crude ABC books of my childhood thrilled me— and I would—I believe—better appreciate some of the little child's way of interpreting life. My first reading lessons were from those books. I learned to recognize letters and a few words.

I started to school when I was almost seven years old. The schoolhouse was built of logs and had two doors, one in the east and one in the west. These doors were both left open in warm weather but the east door was kept shut in winter and over it was hung the blackboard. This was made of smooth boards nailed on battens, like a barn door, and the smooth side painted black. Several incidents in my school experience are still clear in my memory, one especially, is about my hat. My hat was evidently one my brother had worn almost out and left to me. It had no brim but tapered from the lower edge to the top. At the top was a hole—I don't remember how the hole got there, but I do remember that the boy sitting behind me would often pull my hair which stuck through that hole.

---

[41] George Byron (1788-1824). English writer and poet.

My earliest experiences at school were a curious mixture of loneliness, fear, and pleasure. I was of very timid nature, afraid of strangers, even of the large pupils. I remember one day, it must have been near Christmas, a large boy had a toy pistol at school with which he frightened me. I ran down the lane from the school to get away from him, and when I thought he was gone and I was coming back, he jumped out from a fence corner and snapped the toy pistol at me, giving me a great fright. I remember one day my brother was kept at home for something and I was sent to school by myself. I felt so lonely before I got to school it seemed I couldn't bear to go on alone. I started back home but was afraid to go home for fear my mother would punish me. She was no person to trifle with when she decided one of her offspring ought to do something. I stopped as close to the house as I thought safe and sat down on a bridge across a ditch. I could look through the crack in the fence and see our house. I got so homesick I began to cry. My mother heard me and at once decided what the trouble was. I was brought to the house without ceremony or sympathy. I escaped a spanking but was set at hulling walnuts. If you never had to hull walnuts when you were about seven, you can't imagine my predicament. I wished a thousand times that day I had gone on to school.

My first school was in Clary District in Saline County. When I was about eight or nine, we moved into Hamilton County and I started to school in Pleasant Grove District, sometimes called Douglass, and also The Shed. The reason for this last name, I presume, was the fact that a large shed which was used as a place of worship stood not far from the school in a cleared place in the woods.

At this second school I soon began to like to go to school and began to like the lessons and to enjoy reading the few books we had. At about this time I became afflicted with an ailment the doctor called curvature of the spine, which rendered me almost helpless most of the time, and, of course, prevented me from going to school. My ailment caused me to suffer much pain at times, often keeping me awake all night. I remember on one occasion my parents became so alarmed that the relatives and neighbors were called in. I must have been delirious or unconscious, for I remember that it seemed to me I suddenly awoke to find a lot of people standing round my bed and hear someone say: "he has come to."

During all this time that I couldn't go to school my mother taught me to read and write. Someone gave me a book of fairy tales which I read over and over. The first schoolbooks we had in our home were McGuff's [McGuffey] Readers, Watson's Speller, and White's Intermediate Arithmetic.

At Douglass or Pleasant Grove or The Shed I was very fortunate in my teachers for what time I did get to go to school. My first teacher in this school was a Mr. Anderson Porter, knowing the neighborhood as "Little Anderson." Then there was Mr. Z.W. Young, Warren Young. This teacher was a very fine man and an excellent school teacher. He inspired me with a great desire to get an education. I remember distinctly how he taught us the multiplication table. He would take three units of a table—say the sevens—and would go over these backward and forward over and over until we had learned them. Then he would say something like this—"Now, it seems that you know these, but by tomorrow or next week, if you were to [words missing] … would go on to urge us to go over them again and again while we were at home going about our chores or sitting around the fire. I doubt if Mr. Young ever read a book on psychology and yet he was using some very important psychological principles in teaching. And besides his scientific teaching he was inspiring us to go ahead on our own and do our learning without help.

During the winter of 1889 my father bought a farm four miles east of the village of Broughton and we moved to a new home. I left Mr. Young for good but his influence on me was never lost.

But while losing the presence of Mr. Young, I gained much by the move for my new school teacher proved to be a man of rare strength of character, ability, and personality. His name was Arthur Dawes and he was to yield a greater influence in my life than probably any other person I ever knew. He became my hero in every way. Even his bodily defects seemed to me to be marks of superiority, and I unconsciously tried to imitate them. He aroused in me a love for the best literature and all other branches of learning. He was not a finished scholar, but was a clear thinker and a thorough teacher. I believe he was one of the best teachers of reading I ever knew. He refused to pass by a single thought in a lesson until it was thoroughly understood by every pupil if possible. I often recall that Lincoln said, "All I am or hope to be, I owe to my angel mother." While I feel that I owe much, very much for anything of true worth which I am to my mother, I must say that whatever I have accomplished in my chosen life's work, which is nearing completion, I owe to the inspiration of my teachers, and most especially to Arthur Dawes.

So much of my life has been occupied with school teaching that I am constrained to say a few things in connection with my experiences along that line. I can hardly remember when I wasn't fired with a great desire to learn—to get an education. I had no definite plans or ideas about it for a long time but from my earliest recollections about such things, books and stories in books—information to be derived from books had a peculiar attraction for me. When I finally got able to go to school, which was after I was thirteen or fourteen, I was not a star pupil particularly, in fact, I think I was just a very ordinary pupil. But somewhere about that age I somehow got it definitely in my mind that I wanted to be a school teacher. I had one teacher—in a summer school—I being considered a sort of cripple was allowed to go to school while my older brother, who was strong, had to help with the farm work. Well, this teacher talked to me about what I wanted to do when I grew up, and I remember saying to him one evening as we walked along the road on the way home after school that if I thought I could ever learn enough and could get education enough I would like to be a school teacher. This teacher told me he thought it would be an easy matter for me to be able to get a certificate to teach as soon as I was old enough to be admitted to the examination. I thought a lot about what he said and wondered if it could be possible.

During the winter of 1889, a week or two before

Christmas, we moved to a new place and I started to school to a new teacher, the Mr. Dawes I mentioned before. This teacher took a special interest in me, as he did in all his pupils, and he soon aroused in me a greater desire to learn and to be a teacher. He used to come to our house to spend the night and would sit by the big open fireplace and exchange stories and experiences with my parents. He would read to us children from choice literature. I remember it was through such associations with Mr. Dawes that I became acquainted with Snow Bound, Evangeline, and many other selections from the best literature. During the winter of 1893-1894 Mr. Dawes was elected tax collector in our township and he asked me if I would assist him in collecting the taxes.

Of course, I gladly accepted and went to live at his house, went to school at the village school where he was principal and worked for him after school and evenings helping collect the taxes. In the evenings, when such work was done for the day, Mr. Dawes would sit with me by the fire and read from some good book or poem, always from the…. [lines missing].

During the summer of 1894 I attended a review school for advanced pupils and teachers in the local village. The teacher was Mr. M. L. Clark, and the students included some of the county's leading schoolteachers. In addition to the common branches included in the requirements for second grade certificate I studied algebra. The school continued for six weeks and I derived a lot of good in learning and inspiration.

On March 9, 1895, I entered the county examination for second grade certificate, passed with good grades and received a second-grade certificate, qualifying me as a teacher. I don't know what finally became of that first certificate of mine, but I often told folks I wore it out showing it to people. I failed to get a school to teach the first year, and as teachers were required to take an examination each year as long as they held only a second-grade certificate, I entered the county examination again in 1896. This time I was employed to teach at Hickory Corner school in my home district.

There are a few things in my experience as a

schoolteacher, which, as they seem to me, stand out clear in their contribution to whatever success I have attained. And while I know anything, everything I have accomplished in my chosen work is very small and insignificant when compared with what I might have done—or with what some other person might have done, yet I hardly know whether or not I could do better under the circumstances if it were possible for me to start over.

Occasionally I get a chance to talk about different phases of life and its problems and sometimes I say that I believe I have been a very fortunate person. In all my life I have been motivated by two great desires and I can truthfully say that in a great measure I have attained both. One of these desires was to be a good teacher. Just how good a teacher I was is probably not for me to say, but it is a source of gratification to me that I have succeeded in reaching some of the better positions open to schoolteachers in my county. I have … [words missing] the fact that I hold no college degree and did not even attend college until after I was almost forty years old. I realize it is difficult for me to say this without leaving the feeling that I am boasting about it, but truly, nothing is quite so mortifying to me as to have to admit that I never even attended high school.

I began teaching at Hickory Corner in September 1896. From the start I believe I was fully aware of the immense responsibilities heaped upon a school teacher. I tried from the very start to make careful preparation of every lesson. I remember that I often wrote down the questions that I expected to use in the third reader lesson. I had the best lesson helps available at that time, the School News, a journal for teachers, published at Taylorville, Illinois. In this school journal were published articles on the different subjects taught in the grade schools, written usually, by teachers in the different state normal school. I was a subscriber to this journal for twelve years and had every number for the entire dozen years.

My experience as a teacher covers a period of almost fifty years. Counting the time that I served as County Superintendent of Schools it amounts to more than fifty years. I did not teach continuously all that time. I worked at other jobs about seven years, leaving something less than fifty years as teacher. A few selections of literature I studied stands out prominently as having exerted a great influence on my life and work as a teacher. Years ago, I read the biography of Edmund Burke, the great Irish leader in the English Parliament.[42] Burke was a poor boy with apparently little chance of ever becoming a great man. He got a job, as I remember, as janitor for a noted law firm in London. It is said that in a few years the lawyers discovered that the young janitor knew more about the law and the law cases handled by the firm than many of the lawyers. It developed that Burke had a passion for learning everything about all the things that entered into his experience that it was possible for him to learn. When I read that I pondered: "Why shouldn't I try to learn everything possible about the work I am trying to do?"

So, I set out to learn everything I could about every school subject I tried to teach. If it was American History, I secured high school and college textbooks and studied them in connection with the lessons as I came to them in my daily work. I followed the same course in geography, arithmetic and the other studies. This led me into Ancient, Medieval, and Modern World history; into algebra, geometry, and trigonometry; into physical geography and astronomy. Later when I had an opportunity to go to college, I really astonished myself at the amount of work I was able to do.

In my work as superintendent of schools the most distressing thing I meet is the apparent lack of earnest hard individual study among our school teachers. It seems many of them have acquired the notion that they cannot engage in prolonged hard study without attending school, and having their work assigned to them by a teacher. I believe the attitude of our normal schools, colleges, and universities is largely responsible

---

[42] Edmund Burke (1729-1797). Author and member of English Parliament.

for a great deal of this attitude of mind among school teachers. Teachers have learned that only that part of their education and training acquired under the direct supervision of some institution of higher learning ever amounts to anything as far as securing for them recognition. A teacher's ability to teach, it seems, is measured almost entirely by the number of semester hours of work he or she has had in certain required subjects. The worst effect of such a policy is to induce in teachers minds the attitude that any hard earnest study they do at home or in their own study rooms is so much time wasted.

Teaching school, I believe, was harder for me than for many people. I was rather timid by nature, and the work of organizing a large group of young people of various ages was very trying on me at times. Country schools of fifty years ago, that is, in the late [18]90's, were crowded with thirty-five to fifty boys and girls. There were few high schools in our county, in fact, only one, and the older boys and girls continued in the grades until they become twenty-one years old, or more, until they dropped out of school.

In many communities the standards of conduct among young people were not very high and a school teacher was very apt to have trouble somewhere in his experience if he tried to maintain order and discipline among his pupils. And quite often a teacher would find that the folks in his district, instead of landing him their sympathy and aid, seemed to take a fierce delight in his troubles and even sometimes encouraged the big boys to give trouble. In meeting such conditions, I was always at more or less a handicap. I did have one quality that sustained me at all times. I had a dogged determination to see a task through no matter how hard the going out. Many bits of literature that stuck to me like beggar ticks helped me. I remember one or two: "our greatest glory is not in never falling, but in rising every time we fall," and "Hard times kill little people; they make big people."

There's too much to this story of my experiences as a teacher to try to tell it all here. One or two other things I should like to mention however as contributing to what little success I have had. I always had, or soon acquired, an intense love of the theory of teaching. The principles underlying child growth and development. The influences that worked for the development of the best, most genuine personality became the most interesting phase of study I could find. I have gradually, through my years of study, come to the belief that what we call regeneration is the result of education—genuine education. The scriptures say "Train up a child in the way he should go and when he is old, he will not depart from it." He will not depart from it if his education has been of the right sort. He has become a different person—different from what the kind of person who acts in a certain way—the right way. He doesn't do things that seem always expedient—but what he feels and knows are right. That conviction and belief thoroughly grounded in me, I feel, has been a great factor in my success as a teacher.

Appendix II

Genetic Genealogy of the Allen Family

Mark W. Allen, PhD

The surname Allen is a common one with many different origins. Some Allens trace their ancestry to Normandy as an Allen was associated with the Norman Conquest. The name also developed in Scotland, Ireland, and England in many times and places. Since the surname is so common it is difficult to trace beyond a few hundred years through traditional genealogy sources. Fortunately, recent years have seen the development of incredible strides in the use of genetic analyses for the purposes of genealogy. This appendix summarizes the results of DNA tests for Howard W. Allen and his son Mark W. Allen. It presents the current time estimates and posited relationships as of August, 2022. Refinements of genetic testing and future tests are sure to lead to significant changes, this is an on-going process.

Autosomal DNA Results

Autosomal DNA is from the 22 pairs of autosomal (non-sex) chromosomes that individuals inherit from their parents (one of the pair from the father, the other from the mother). Our autosomal DNA represents a tremendous mixture of human genes since the origin of our species (*Homo sapiens sapiens*) roughly 200,000 years ago in Africa. Autosomal DNA is very useful for obtaining a broad look at one's heritage, but it can only identify genetic relatives within the last five or six generations. Because of recombination during sex cell production and since only half of a parent's chromosome pair are passed on to a child, only grandparents and parents are absolutely guaranteed to have passed on genes to descendants. The further back an ancestor sits on the family tree, the less likely that a descendant shares DNA.

Howard Allen's Ancestry autosomal test, as well as his tested close relatives, shows a consistent dominance of DNA common to the British Isles indicating that his recent ancestors over the past five or six generations share that origin. Ancestry provides the following estimates for his autosomal DNA: 42% England and Northwestern Europe, 41% Scotland, 14% Ireland, 2% Wales, and 1% Norway. It further estimates that one parent (likely his mother) provided roughly two-thirds of his Scottish and Irish ancestry and the other (likely his father) provided about two-thirds of his English and Northwestern Europe ancestry. This autosomal test also identifies DNA communities that are likely to represent the places and cultural groups of one's ancestors over the past few centuries. Howard is connected to four such communities: Eastern North Carolina Settlers; Lower Midwest and Virginia Settlers; Scottish Lowlands, Northern England and Northern Ireland; and Southern Midwestern Settlers.

Howard also has autosomal test results from Family Tree DNA which are presented differently: 54% England, Wales, and Scotland; 26% Ireland; and 20% Central Europe. This company also provides a breakdown of autosomal DNA according to ancient European origins. Howard Allen's results are 6% Metal Age Invader (i.e. Bronze and Iron Age), 43% Farmer (Neolithic populations that migrated from the Near East to Central Europe), 51% Hunter-Gatherer (genes from the earlier inhabitants of Europe back to 40,000 years ago), and 0% non-European.

It should be noted, however, that these popular autosomal tests are broad estimates only and the reality is that everybody has genes from a wide range of areas and ancestral populations. For example, while Mark Allen's own autosomal results from both FTDNA and Ancestry tests show about 87% British Isles and 13%

Scandinavian, a more detailed look at his genetic information reveals small percentages of Native American, African, South Asian, and other various populations. Almost everyone of British Isles descent (and elsewhere) would find the same thing if they were to examine their own autosomal DNA results more deeply. Humans of the past were mobile, and genes have always been widely mixed across different groups of people. Looking for "pure" strains of humans is a lost cause, there are none except perhaps the most isolated populations up to a few centuries ago.

Mitochondrial DNA Results

The X and Y sex chromosomes (XX = female, XY = male) provide a unique opportunity for genetic genealogical research. Mitochondrial DNA is only passed on from a mother to her children through her X chromosome. This DNA is not subject to natural selection and changes only due to mutations which occur rarely. It thus provides an ideal way to trace the long-term maternal line of an individual. The problem is that because it changes so slowly it is not very useful for identifying ancestors from the recent past--matches could represent common ancestors from a few generations ago or thousands of years ago. On the other hand, it does permit tracing maternal genetic heritage back to the origin of the species. This can be thought of as a tree that spreads branches through time as new mutations developed. The major branches of the tree are known as haplogroups.

Howard Allen's mitochondrial DNA has been determined through a test with Family Tree DNA. This of course represents what he inherited from his mother, Helen Marie Allen (nee Wilson). She in turn, inherited it from her mother Edith Floy Wilson (nee Brinkley), who inherited it from her mother Martha Ann Brinkley (nee Hall), who inherited if from her mother Mary J. Hall (nee Moore), who inherited it from her mother (who may be Emily Russell who lived approximately 1800-1850, mother unknown), and so on back to the origin of anatomically modern humans around 200,000 years ago.

The results of this test are Haplogroup J1b1a1-T146C!, and according to Family Tree DNA:

> The mitochondrial haplogroup J contains several sub-lineages. The original haplogroup J originated in the Near East approximately 50,000 years ago. Within Europe, sub-lineages of haplogroup J have distinct and interesting distributions . . . throughout Europe, but at a relatively low frequency. Haplogroup J is generally considered one of the prominent lineages that was part of the Neolithic spread of agriculture into Europe from the Near East beginning approximately 10,000 years ago (https://www.familytreedna.com/my/mtdna-migration-map/).

YDNA Results

The other type of sex chromosome DNA analysis is YDNA, passed on from father to son through the Y chromosome. This type of DNA mutates much more frequently than mitochondrial DNA and since over the past millennium or so Western civilization practiced patrilineal descent (inheriting the surname from the paternal side), it provides a unique ability to provide genealogical information. Surnames only developed in Europe around 700 years ago as medieval lords sought to improve their ability to tax people, but the line of male ancestors can be traced back much deeper than that. There is roughly a 16% chance that a son will have a mutation difference from his father. Such a mutation in the YDNA means that a son has a variant from his father. Through time these variants become branches or subclades of haplogroups.

YDNA can be assessed through two different measures through Family Tree DNA. One is STR (short tandem repeat) tests. These can be done at different levels: 12 STR, 25 STR, 37 STR, 67 STR, or 111 STR. These refer to the number of panels that are examined for repeating strands of nucleotides (built from strands of the four building blocks of DNA: A, C, G, T) that form DNA segments. These panels have been identified as being particularly useful for tracing haplogroups. Matches with individuals at the lower levels (12 or 25 STR) are not really that useful as they will only identify a major branch of the YDNA tree, one that dates back well over 10,000 years and perhaps as much as 50,000 or more. The company no longer provides tests at this low level of resolution. The higher-level tests provide a much more recent haplogroup. It can help to identify matches with the same surname as the tester, as well as other close male relatives.

The second YDNA test available through FTDNA is called Big Y 700 and it examines thousands of known YDNA branch markers. It analyzes millions of strands of DNA Single Nucleotide Polymorphisms (SNPs) which are multiple varieties of strands of nucleotides. It provides a very detailed picture of a man's YDNA and if enough closely related men have also tested it can provide a very detailed genealogical lineage that can bridge the gap between historic documents and the more distant past, much older than the development of surnames.

Both Howard Wilson Allen and Mark Wilson Allen have had the 111 STR level of YDNA testing and have an exact match for all 111 markers. They also both match with two other individuals as of August 2022. This includes another Allen at six steps of genetic distance (a step is not the same thing as a generation). He has been identified through consultation with his family and Merritt Robert's (1985) family history as a descendant of Gideon Allen's oldest son, James Allen (see Chapter One). He and Mark are both 6th great grandsons of Gideon. The match and some of his family still live in Johnston County, North Carolina. Allens have thus been in the same location that Gideon lived in some two hundred years after Josiah Allen left for Tennessee around 1820. The second match at the 111 STR level has an unknown father, but he was definitely an Allen. He is five steps of genetic distance from both Howard and Mark, thus perhaps a bit closer than the Allen match with a known paternal lineage.

All four of these men have also been tested with the Big Y 700 method. This has resulted in the creation of two new branches of Allen men under haplogroup R-Z29008 which dates to around 1,300 years ago. The oldest branch has been assigned R-FTB81068. It originated roughly 3000 years ago, but this is a statistical approximation. If the traditional genealogy documents for Gideon Allen and his sons are correct, Gideon himself was most likely R-FTB81068 since all of his descendants derive from this haplogroup. The two men who match with Howard and Mark at the 111 STR level with five and six steps of genetic distance are both assigned to this branch as of September 2022. Additional Big Y 700 tests of related men or further review of their variants will likely break them into yet unidentified branches. The current evidence suggests they are both descendants of Gideon's oldest son James Allen (~1740-1787), while Howard and Mark descend from Gideon's son John Allen (~1747-1796).

The second thus far identified branch under R-Z29008 originated only around 100 years ago (+/- 50 years) and has been identified as R-FTB80139. It originated most likely in Omar Allen, but the mutation could have arisen in Howard Wilson Allen, Howard Henderson Allen, or even William Bright Allen. Also worth noting is that Mark and Howard have a single SNP mutation difference, which happens as noted earlier in about 16% of male offspring.

Specifically, at position 5193997 Howard has a "G" nucleotide, while Mark has a "C."

Just as with STR testing, the Big Y 700 test provides genetic matches with other men who have been tested. FTDNA defines a Big Y DNA match as having 30 or fewer SNP differences. Howard has 19 such matches with the following surnames besides his Allen matches: Bateman, Carrell, Carroll, Daly, Daley, Gaston, Gleason, Glisson, Hally, Hawley, Mackey, Miller, and Treacy. Clearly, several of them are cases of different spellings that developed through time. A few identify their earliest known paternal ancestor as American, but most identify him as originating in Ireland. Interestingly, the slight difference in just one SNP between Howard and Mark means that Mark has only 16 matches with the following surnames: Bateman, Bunn, Carrell, Carroll, Daley, Gaston, Glisson, Hally, Hawley, Miller, and Treacy. All of these tested men share R-Z29008 as a common ancestor who again lived about 1,300 years ago.

The best way to visualize this is to think of branches of the tree of literally mankind, going back to the common male ancestor of the species in Africa some 200,000 years ago. Our Allen paternal line belongs to the major Haplogroup R. It is very common among males of European descent but is also found today among men in Central Asia and South Asia as well as parts of Africa. It is estimated to have developed with an individual from the Upper Paleolithic period around 27,000 years ago. It is helpful to think of each of these haplogroup names as an individual who had a new variant of YDNA from his father--a new mutation.

Our paternal line has the following major branches moving through time from oldest branch to youngest:

R-M207>R-M173>**R-M343**>R-L754>R-L389>R-P297>**R-M269**>R-L23>R-L51>R-P310>R-L51>**R-P312**>R-Z290>**R-**

L21>R-S552>R-DF13>R-ZZ10-1>R-Z16423>**R-Z255**>R-Z16437>**R-A557**>**R-A10895**>**R-Z29008**>R-FTB81068>R-FTB80139.

Rather than summarize each of these major branches, just some of the key haplogroups (those in bold) are discussed here to show the gradual movement of our paternal ancestor from Asia to the British Isles and eventually North America. All time estimates are those provided by Family Tree DNA as of September 2022, and these will be refined as more data become available. The development of haplogroup R-M343 (which used to be known as simply R1b) is of major consequence. This is the most frequent YDNA among men of Western Europe today but is found in other areas as well. It probably developed around 19,000 (+/- 2,500) years ago in Western Asia.

Haplogroup R-M269 (used to be known as R1b1a1a2) is the most common European haplogroup. It now has over 22,000 different branches. Over 90% of Welsh men are R-M269, while only about 20% of men in Eastern Europe are in the group. Generally, it declines in frequency from west to east among modern European men. It developed most likely during the Neolithic period around 6,350 (+/- 950) years ago. This period was when agriculture and pastoralism were spreading out of the Near East, but there is evidence that the haplogroup first appeared in Eastern European or Western Asian hunter-gatherers in the steppes rather than Mesopotamian farmers. It expanded rapidly westwards, accelerated by the major advantage of horses for transportation and their use in warfare.

Haplogroup R-P312 likely developed in the Rhine Basin of Germany during the Early Bronze Age around 4,800 (+/- 700) years ago. It moved westwards into Western Europe. Out of this branched Haplogroup R-L21 which is associated with the expansion of Celtic populations into the British Islands, France, and Spain. The expansion of these Metal Age invaders was at the cost of earlier inhabitants of these regions. Essentially, earlier forms of YDNA dropped down to 10% or less of their former levels. However, mitochondrial DNA haplogroups did not change significantly, suggesting that the invaders removed the male competition and incorporated indigenous women into their own societies. Bronze weapons would have been a major advantage for the descendants of R-L21 and they seem to have used them ruthlessly. It formed shortly after R-P312, roughly 4,600 (+/- 650) years ago. The next several haplogroups in our Allen paternal line continued the expansion into the British Islands.

Haplogroup R-Z255 is commonly known as the Irish Sea Haplogroup. It formed about 2,100 (+/- 350) years ago and is found today in Great Britain, France, Norway, and Sweden, but is most frequent along the coasts of the Irish Sea. Many of the Irish Kings of Leinster were in this haplogroup. The Scandinavian men with the Irish Sea variant are thought to be mainly the results of slaves taken from Britain by raiding Vikings, though surely some men were willing recruits.

Haplogroup R-A557 dates to the early Medieval Period, around 1,700 (+/- 350) years ago. It likely originated in Ireland. A century or two later, Haplogroup R-A10895 developed in Ireland. As noted earlier, haplogroup R-Z29008 dates to 1,300 (+/- 350) years ago and is the ancestor of all of the Big Y 700 matches noted above for Howard and Mark.

Figure 1 is taken from a tool available for Big Y DNA testers through FTDNA to visualize the results of their tests. It is called a time tree and shows the most recent part of the tree for Howard and Mark Allen.

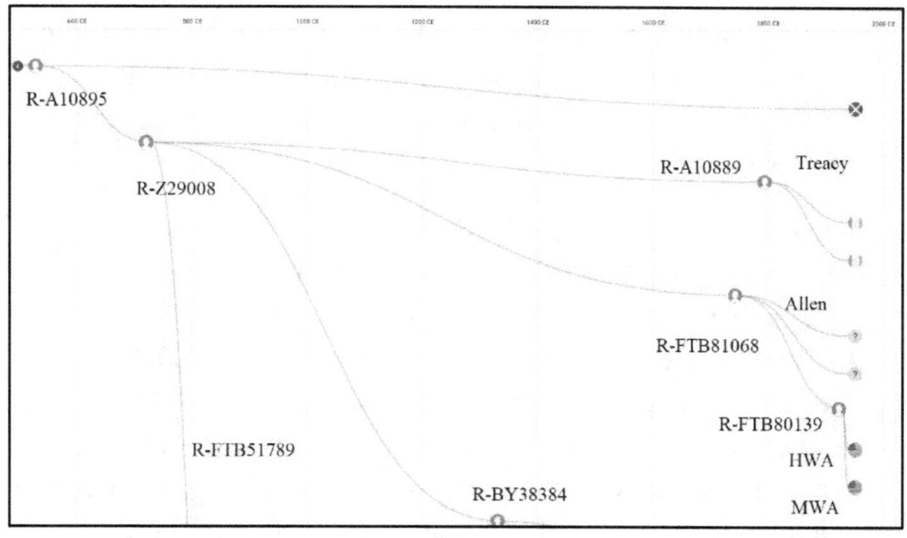

Figure 1. Time Tree for some of the descendants of ancestor R-Z29008 who lived around 1,300 years ago. He was a descendant of ancestor R-A10895 who lived around 1,500 years ago. At least four lines descend from R-Z29008. One of these lines led to R-A10889, an ancestor of two men surnamed Treacy who trace their oldest known paternal ancestor to Ireland. R-FTB81068 is likely Gideon Allen, born around 1720. Three identified lines descend from him. RFTB-80139 developed in the descendants of Gideon's son John Allen (born around 1747) around 100 years ago and most likely originated in Omar Allen. Both Howard and Mark Allen belong to this haplogroup. The other two lines descending from Gideon are currently unnamed (represented by question marks) and belong to the two other Allen relatives who have taken Big Y 700 tests. They most likely descend from a different son of Gideon Allen. R-FTB51789 and R-BY38384 are lines that lead to other descendants of ancestor R-Z29008, with most testers on these tracing back to oldest known paternal ancestors in Ireland.

Over time, other males who descend from ancestor R-Z9008 are going to get tested at the Big Y DNA level. Some of these will trace their surname to Allen, but most will not. It is hoped that eventually a bridge will be established that links Gideon Allen to our Irish ancestors and insight might be gained as to when our paternal line split from the other surnames that are Big Y 700 matches.

Gideon may have self-identified as Irish when he showed up in Johnston County, North Carolina by 1747. However, it seems unlikely that he did for a few reasons. First, mass migration from Northern Ireland to America had not yet begun by 1700-1725 when he was likely born. Most of the early settlers of North Carolina were English coming from the colony of Virginia in search of cheap land and greater independence. Second, Gideon built a fair amount of wealth within a short period of time, suggesting that he had sufficient resources to purchase numerous parcels of land and at least some slaves, as well as the capital to run a ferry on the Cape Fear River just west of Johnston County as far back as 1755. Third, his sons and grandsons evidently intermarried with the prominent Smith family that ran the ferry over the Neuse River starting in 1759, and who largely established the important tobacco shipping town of Smithfield which became the Johnston County seat in 1777. The Smiths were English who came to the area from Virginia by the late 1730s (see Appendix III for details on Gideon Allen and the Smiths). It seems unlikely that a recent Irish immigrant would be so close to the most notable family in the county. It is important to remember that around 1,000 years passed between Irish ancestor R-Z29008 and the birth of Gideon Allen, plenty of time for an ancestor to migrate to England, Scotland, or elsewhere.

We are thus left with an interesting mystery. Where did Gideon come from? Was he born in England, Virginia, coastal North Carolina, or somewhere else? Hopefully, answers to these questions may be partially answered by further YDNA testing to narrow the gap between a Medieval Irishman and Gideon of

Johnston County, North Carolina who founded a numerous branch of American Allens. Just going back to individuals born by 1960, there are at least 3,000 descendants who have thus far been identified by Merrit Roberts (1985) and recent research by another genealogist.

APPENDIX III

Notes on Gideon Allen Ferryman and a
Legal Dispute Over Dawson's Ferry

Mark W. Allen, PhD

According to the research of Merritt Roberts in his book *Roberts-Allen Families and Related Families*, Gideon Allen "first appeared in the records of Johnston County in 1748."[1] The county was formed in 1746, so he was a relatively early settler. Roberts notes that he sold and bought land in the county from 1750 to 1755, though details are missing due to lost land deeds from 1747-1760. However, I did find a petition by Gideon for a warrant of 100 acres to the colonial government in New Bern dated April 11, 1749. Other petitions from that session include those of John Smith (more on him below) and two other men with the surname Dees.[2] The location for these warrants is denoted in the records as "D_o" rather than the full name of the appropriate county as it was for the majority of filed petitions. Since both Smith and Dees are names later associated with Gideon's land transactions in Johnston County, it is strong evidence that the abbreviation was for Johnston County.

A few miles southwest of the Johnston County seat of Smithfield in the area between Hannah and Mill Creeks is the unincorporated community known as Allens Crossroads (Figure 1). While it is not certain that Gideon himself owned land here, it is documented that his descendants over the next many generations did. There are several 19th Century cemeteries with known Allen graves and at least two of them are named after Allens. While there are no known graves from the 18th Century, Gideon's son John Allen (1740-1796) was given land by John Smith in 1775 on Mill Creek, and John's son William Allen (~1774-1832) is one of many Allens that owned land along Hannah and Mill Creeks. Allens Crossroad may thus be viewed as a core area of our Allen ancestors by the late 18th Century. Quite likely, Josiah Allen (1798-1855) of Hamilton County, Illinois was born in the vicinity of Allens Crossroads.

Roberts also notes that Gideon was involved in buying and selling land in Cumberland County along the Cape Fear River from 1755-1760, but he incorrectly concludes that there is no evidence that he ever lived there. This county (now Harnett) bordered Johnston County to the west and is about four miles southwest of Allens Crossroads. He certainly resided in Cumberland County no later than 1756 as proved by his second appearance in the *Colonial Records of North Carolina*. On March 19, 1756 in New Bern, the Council appointed new justices for Cumberland County and stipulated that Gideon and four other men be *removed* from that position, implying of course that he served in that role prior to that spring.[7] This was a sign of trouble to come for Gideon as he soon got into a legal conflict with William Dawson, Justice of the Peace and eldest son of Jeffrey (Geoffrey) Dawson. The elder Dawson was an early Welsh settler in the county and the founder of Dawson's Ferry over the Cape Fear River just east of the county courthouse. The Dawsons also ran a tavern near the courthouse.

However, Roberts neglects to mention or failed to discover the key reason that Gideon purchased land in Cumberland County in 1755. I discovered the motive when I conducted a Google search for Gideon Allen and turned up a reference to him in an article on the colonial ferries of North Carolina. It noted that Gideon Allen was paid by the proceeds of a two-penny tax to keep a public ferry in Cumberland County for one year.[3] Intrigued, I followed this up by tracking down the provided reference, the July 1757 minutes from the Cumberland Court of Pleas and Quarter Sessions.[4]

My transcription of the relevant hand-written minutes is:

The court ordered that there of two pence taxable laid on the taxable in this County in order to pay Gideon Allen ten pounds proclamation money in order that he shall keep free Ferry for all persons During the continuance of court musters and collections for one year.

When the justices reconvened the next day, it seems they had a change of heart:

The Court ordered that the the [sic] tax of two penys p(?) taxable that were to be levied on the inhabitants of this county to pay Gideon Allen (illegible word) for keeping free Ferry in (illegible word) publik(?) (illegible word) is made(?) void—by order of said Court.

While the illegible words in the court minutes make this interpretation uncertain, subsequent events suggest that the ferry license was taken away from Gideon by the court, perhaps due to the machinations of

William Dawson who clearly wanted the ferry back under family control, and who still owned the tavern and land on the west side of the river.

Most likely Gideon was attempting to renew the ferry license when it was apparently denied by the court. Cumberland County deeds obtained from the county Register of Deeds Book 1 show that Gideon and his wife Elizabeth purchased land along the Cape Fear River from Johnathan and Ruth Lewelling (also spelled Lewellyn in some documents) on September 20, 1755.[5]

The first deed begins: *"This Indenture made the twentieth day of September in the year of our Lord one thousand seven hundred and fifty five between Jonathan Lewelling of Cumberland County in the Province of North Carolina, Joyner, of the one part, and Gideon Allen of the County and Province aforesaid **Ferryman** (bold added) of the other part . . . (ineligible word) . . . that whereas Thomas Armstrong by force and virtue of his majestice [sic] letter patent bearing date the 1st June ano Domina 1740 became lawfully seized . . . (several ineligible words) . . . in three hundred acres of land lying and being in said County of Cumberland, formerly called Bladen County, and on the Est. side of the N.W. Branch of Cape Fear River beginning at Jeffrey Dawsons lower corner"*.

The rest of the deed states that William Dawson had earlier purchased the land from Armstrong on August 29, 1746 and subsequently sold it to Jonathan Lewelling on September 20, 1750. Gideon paid Lewelling 82£ for it. A second transaction between Gideon and the Lewellings was made on that same fall day of 1755. He paid 28£ for 100 acres which had originally been patented by Jeffrey Dawson December 21, 1741, and later transferred to his son William. The Lewellings had purchased it from William five years earlier on September 10, 1750.

These documents identify Gideon as a ferry operator before the fall of 1755, though of course it is possible that his experience was at a different location. But given these land purchases it seems nearly certain that he was operating Dawson's Ferry by the end of 1755. The ferry and the parcels that Gideon purchased were located at a bend in the Cape Fear River with the land on the eastern side near the modern community of Erwin in Harnett County (formerly Cumberland). A genealogy blog on Dawson family history revealed to me that their namesake ferry was in the vicinity of the Averasboro Civil War battlefield (fought March 15-16, 1865). With that clue, I tracked down its exact location through discovery of an historic district eligibility nomination for the battlefield prepared in 2000. The district was successfully listed on the National Register of Historic Places in May of 2001. It includes the site of Dawson's Ferry, which later became known as Smith's Ferry. The nomination describes it as follows:

The site of the ferry lay directly across from the confluence of the Little River into the Cape Fear River. This ferry was actually established well before the Battle of Averasboro, in 1865. Geoffrey Dawson settled on the east side of the Cape Fear River in 1737. An old Indian trail known as Green's Path was located near Dawson's property. "At some point prior to 1757, the Dawson family established a ferry operation at the mouth of Little River to carry traffic traveling along Green's Path" (Hairr 1999, p.l. Dawson sold the Ferry to Alexander Smith prior to 1761 and became known as Smith's Ferry. It remained a vital crossing until the early twentieth century. Today, it is only a site. There are no recognizable features to distinguish it from other river landings. However, the site was included in an archaeological survey conducted by Ken Robinson for Cumberland County in 1986. The report concluded that the original ferry road (now known as Magruder Road and the natural beach landing are still present (Robinson 1986: p. 108.[6]

Thus far I have not been able to access the two reports (Hairr 1999 and Robinson 1986) cited in the nomination, but it firmly locates Dawson's Ferry at the end of what is now Magruder Road which terminates at the river. Unfortunately, the nomination appears to have errors. If Gideon operated this ferry before 1757, as seems likely from the available documents, his contribution was not credited. Secondly, as noted in detail below, Alexander Smith did not purchase the land and ferry from William Dawson.

In November of 1757 William Dawson and his allies made a bold move to take back control of the ferry a few months after the Cumberland Court first gave Gideon the ferry license only to apparently void it the next day. The minutes of the North Carolina General Assembly House in New Bern record the following:

Friday, 25th November 1757. The House met according to Adjournment. Present as above. Mr. Brown and Mr. Caswell brought up a Bill to prevent excessive and deceitful gaming And a Bill for the better establishing a Ferry on the N.E. side of the N.W. River of Cape Fear, being the place commonly called, or known by the name of Dawson's Ferry and for preventing any other Ferry within (blank space) Miles of the said place and the opposite side of the said River. On motion, ordered the said Bill be read. The same was accordingly read the first time & passed. Then the House adjourned till 3 o'clock in the afternoon.[8]

The bill passed into Law by the Fifth Session of the North Carolina General Assembly in November 1757:

An Act for the better establishing a Ferry on the North-East side of the North -West River of Cape Fear, being the place commonly called or known by the name of Dawson's Ferry.

I. Whereas, the ferry on the North East side of the North West river of Cape Fear, called Dawson's ferry , hath been of long standing; and found very convenient for travellers, and others; and whereas, the land on the North- East side of the said river, where the public road crosses and leads to Yadkin, and so to South Carolina, is the property of William Dawson, who lives thereon; and being desirous that the said ferry should be continued and fixed at the same place; wherefore, for the encouragement of the said William Dawson, and conveniency of all travellers, and to prevent the removing the ferry from the place aforesaid.

II. Be it Enacted, by the Governor, Council, and Assembly, and by the authority of the same, that the said ferry is hereby invested in, and shall from henceforward, be held and deemed the right and property only of the said William Dawson, his heirs and assigns.

III. And be it further Enacted by the authority aforesaid, That the said William Dawson, his heirs or assigns, shall, as soon as conveniently may be, build or provide a good and substantial boat, fit for the transportation of men and horses, and shall maintain and keep the same always in good repair, and give constant attendance at the said ferry; and shall also, for the true performance of the same, at the county court of Cumberland, next after the passing of this Act, enter into bond, with good and sufficient security, to be adjudged and approved by the said Court.

IV. And be it further Enacted by the authority aforesaid, That after a boat is so built or provided, and the security given as aforesaid, That it shall and may be lawful for the said William Dawson, his heirs or assigns, to take and receive from all persons that shall pass over the said ferry, the following rates; that is to say, four pence, proclamation money, for a man and horse, and two pence like money for a footman; and one shilling for each carriage drawn by one or two horses, and for each horse more four pence; and one penny for each steer, cow, hog or sheep.

V. And whereas, part of the road on each side of the said ferry, wants to be cleared and made good; be it Enacted by the authority aforesaid, That the said William Dawson shall, at his own expence, clear the same; that is to say, on the North - East side of the said river, from the ferry to Black river, and so on the South West or opposite side of the said ferry to Cumberland Court-house; and that the same shall afterwards be kept in repair, and maintained by the commissioners and overseers of the district in which the said roads lie.[9]

On Thursday, May 4, 1758 Gideon fought back by filing a petition with the General Assembly:

Mr. Harvey presented to the House a Petition of Gideon Allen, setting forth, That William Dawson obtained the Passing of a Law for establishing to himself a Ferry on the North East of the North West Branch of Cape Fear River, notwithstanding the Petitioner purchased the Land and said Ferry of the said Dawson for a valuable Consideration, and the Petitioner give the said William Dawson Notice to appear.[10]

There is no further mention in the House minutes of this petition, so the outcome is unknown, but it seems likely that it was dropped or rejected soon thereafter. Gideon's name does not appear in the *Colonial Records of North Carolina* again—it was the third and last time that it did.

However, there is no doubt that he quickly began to dispose of his lands on the eastern side of the Cape Fear River. On the 17th of May, 1758, just under two weeks after his petition was presented, he and his wife Elizabeth sold a tract of land at the mouth of the Little River (a tributary flowing into the Cape Fear River just north of Dawson's Ferry) in Cumberland County to William Souther, a merchant of Edgecomb County for 45£. This included "all that lot or parcel of land situated lying and being the County of Cumberland (**excepting the rights of ferry** [bold added] on said land unto the said Gideon Allen and his heir or assigners forever."[11] This was witnessed by Jesse Allen (perhaps a brother of Gideon or other close relative, but unlikely to be Gideon's son Jesse as he would still be a minor at that time) and Thomas Gibson and "proved in open court by the oath of Mr. Thomas Gibson." The deed provides the history of ownership from Jeffrey Dawson to his eldest son William Dawson, and then to Jonathan Lewellen and so is almost certainly the same 300 acres purchased by Gideon in 1755. This sale may indicate that Gideon knew his petition was dead or doomed, but he nonetheless was attempting to hold on to his rights to operate the ferry.

About 20 months later, on March 15, 1760, Gideon "of the County of Cumberland" sold his remaining 100 acres in Cumberland County to John Smith for 40£[12] Both Gideon and Elizabeth attached a seal to this deed. This deed does not mention the ferry at all. Likely, Gideon had lost control of it due to the 1757 law passed by the General Assembly.

The nomination for the Averasboro Battlefield Historic District incorrectly stated that William Dawson sold the ferry to Alexander Smith before 1761, which is the year that Dawson died at about the age of 41. As noted earlier, this is incorrect—John Smith purchased the land on the east side of the river from Gideon in 1760. Smith also bought additional adjoining lands that same year directly from William Dawson and certainly began to run the ferry over the Cape Fear River, and it quickly became known as Smith's Ferry. Alexander Smith, noted in the nomination, is John's son, and he took over its operation in 1764. It was still running well into the 19th Century.

Perhaps some sort of amiable understanding was reached among Gideon, William, and John. It is certainly a more pleasant scenario than the one of Gideon stewing about being done wrong the rest of his life. Regardless, it seems unlikely that Gideon was much upset when William Dawson died shortly after the land and ferry transactions were completed.

A different Smith's Ferry was established on the Neuse River in Johnston County by John Smith in 1759.[13] This site was chosen as the location of a tobacco warehouse as it was the furthest navigable point on the river by 1770. A year later it was chosen for the county courthouse and the settlement started by John and his son John Smith Jr. became Smithfield. It was incorporated as the county seat in 1777. The elder

John Smith (1684-1777) entered the area from Virginia well before it became Johnston County and was probably the most prominent citizen of the region. John ran the Neuse River Smith's Ferry for a few years before turning it over to John Jr. (~1731-1789) in 1762, possibly to enable the elder John to focus on the newly acquired Cumberland County ferry. It must have been confusing for travelers through the region to encounter two Smith's Ferries on two different rivers in two adjacent counties run by members of the same family. There are several clues that suggest that Gideon Allen, his children, and his grandchildren were strongly connected to the Smiths. Besides the land transaction in Cumberland County, several gifts of land were given to Allens by Smiths, such as the gift from John to John Allen in 1775 discussed above. There were likely many intermarriages as children from one surname were often named after individuals from the other over the next two or three generations. It is not a stretch to imagine that Gideon encouraged or influenced the Smiths to get involved in the ferry business. Towards the end of his life, Gideon once again engaged in land transactions in Johnston County. Roberts cites a deed that Gideon bought land on the Neuse River from Jacob Dees in 1765. Other deeds from 1767 record him selling 100 acres on the Neuse River, a slave, and livestock and horses to his son Jesse. Since Gideon does not appear in any more documents, Roberts interprets this as disposal of assets just before his death. No will or probate exists for Gideon or his wife Elizabeth, and their burial location are unknown. It is unknown where Gideon and Elizabeth lived between 1760 and 1765, they may have had earlier land purchases, or might have lived with one of their children. Despite the setback of Dawson's Ferry, Gideon hopefully took satisfaction from the success of his children. They clearly prospered in Johnston County over the next decades and went on to have thousands of Allen and other descendants.

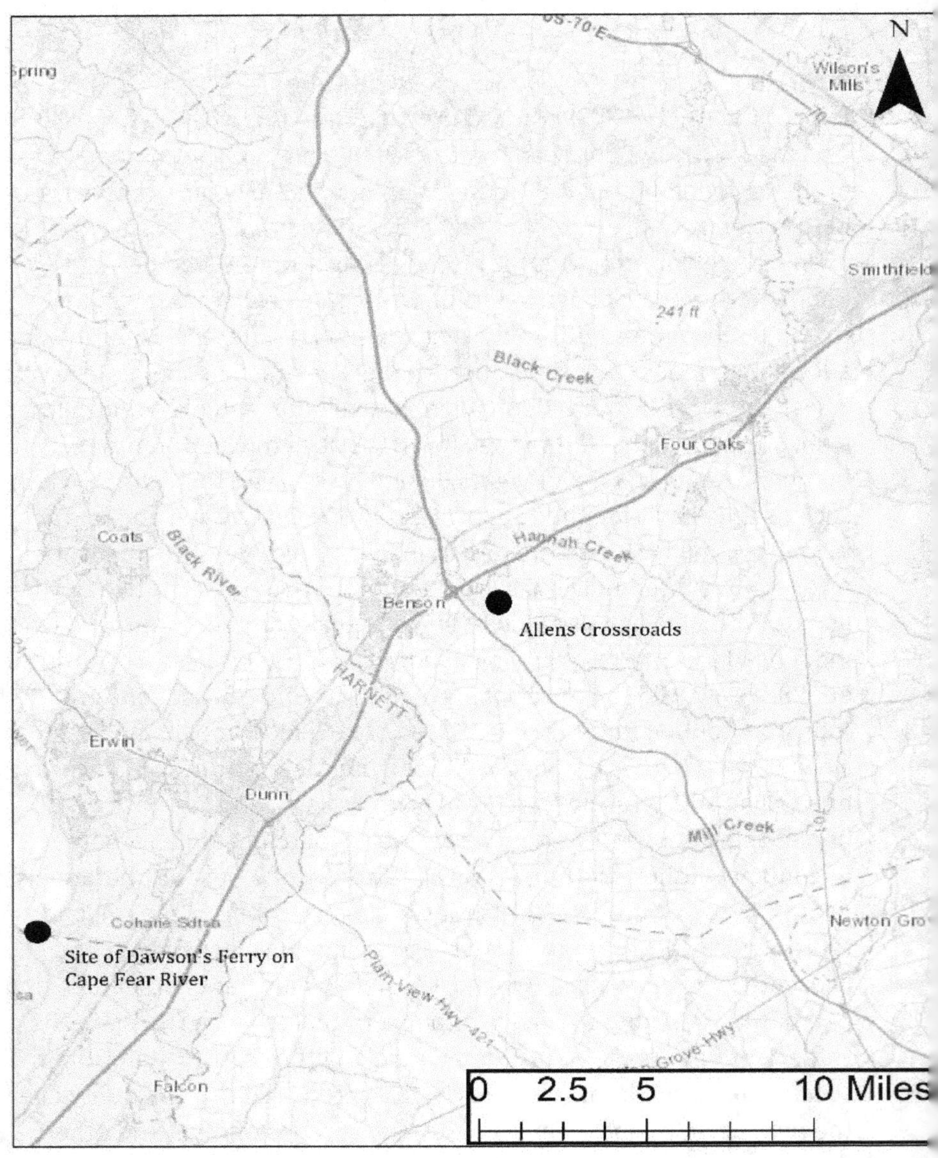

Figure 1. Map Showing Locations of
Allens Crossroad in Johnston
County and Dawson's Ferry in Former
Cumberland County, North Carolina.
Cumberland County is now Harnett
County.

End Notes

[1] Roberts, Merritt E. 1985. *Roberts-Allen Families and Related Families, Davis, Highfill, Rogers*. Olive Press Publications (ISBN 0-933380-3), p.272.

[2] Saunders, William L., (ed.). 1886. *Colonial Records of North Carolina*, Volume 4. Raleigh: Hale, p. 949.

[3] Watson, Alan D. 1974. The Ferry in Colonial North Carolina: A Vital Link in Transportation. *The North Carolina Historical Review* 51:247-260.

[4] Church of Latter Day Saints online Family History Library, Microfilm number 316819, Image Group 7900604.

[5] https://www.ccrod.org

[6] Michael, Michelle A. 2000. Unpublished National Register of Historic Places Registration Form for the Averasboro Battlefield Historic District. Available through the National Register of Historic Places web site.

[7] Saunders, William L. (ed.). 1887. Colonial Records of North Carolina Volume 5. Raleigh: Josephus Daniels, p. 654-665.

[8] Saunders 1987, p. 873-874.

[9] Clark, Walter (ed.). 1906. *The State Record of North Carolina*, Volume 25, pg. 356.

[10] Saunders 1987, p.1012.

[11] Cumberland County Deed Book 1, pages 300-301 (available https://www.ccrod.org).

[12] Cumberland County Deed Book 1, page 365-366 (available https://www.ccrod.org).

[13] https://carolana.com/NC/Towns/Smithfield_NC.html

ABOUT THE AUTHOR

Howard W Allen was born in Dahlgren, Illinois in 1931 and attended the public schools in Dahlgren and graduated from Dahlgren Community High School in 1949. He attended Southern Illinois University in 1949 – 1951. He served stateside in the United States Air Force 1951 – 1952 during the Korean War. He enrolled at the University of Chicago in 1952 where he earned his B. A. In 1954 and his M. A. Degree in 1955. He attended the University of Washington in Seattle from 1955 to 1959 when he received his PhD in American political history. He taught at the University of Akron in Ohio from 1959 to 1962 when he accepted a position at Southern Illinois University in Carbondale, Illinois. In 1964 – 1966, on leave from Southern Illinois University, he served as the Director of Data Recovery and Research Associate in the Inter-University Consortium for Political and Social Research at the University of Michigan. He is the author, co-author or editor of several books and many professional articles. He retired from teaching on January 1, 1998.

www.ingramcontent.com/pod-product-compliance
Lightning Source LLC
Chambersburg PA
CBHW070952250726